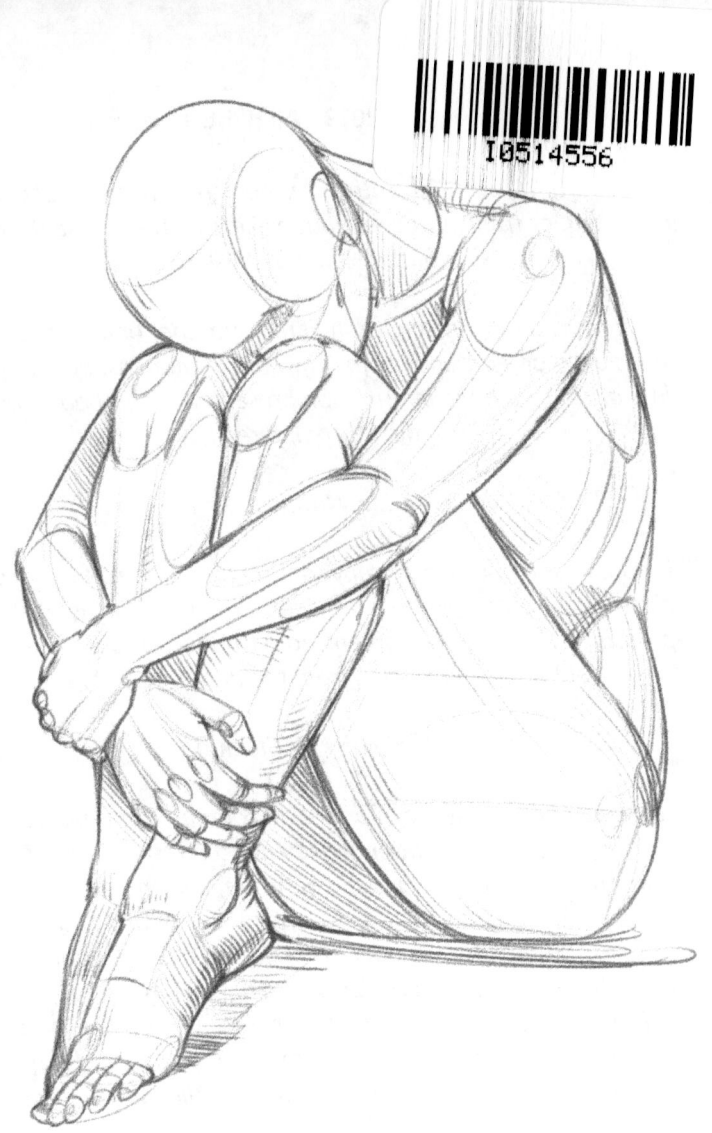

DRAWIX

HANDS AND FEET: Anatomy for Artists Unveiled: Mastering Figure Drawing with Ease and Insider Techniques

© Copyright 2023 - All rights reserved.

The material enclosed within this book may not be replicated, duplicated, or transmitted without explicit written consent from the author or the publisher.

Under no circumstances shall the publisher or author bear responsibility or legal liability for any harm, compensation, or financial loss arising from the information presented in this book, whether directly or indirectly.

Legal Notification:

This book is safeguarded by copyright and is intended for personal use exclusively. Any modification, distribution, sale, utilization, citation, or rephrasing of any part or content from this book is prohibited without obtaining permission from the author or publisher.

Disclaimer Notification:

Please be aware that the information contained in this document is solely intended for educational and entertainmemnt purposes. Every effort has been made to provide accurate, current, dependable, and comprehensive information. No warranties of any nature, either express or implied, are provided. Readers acknowledge that the author is not engaged in the provision of legal, financial, medical, or professional advice. The content in this book has been sourced from various references. It is advisable to consult a licensed professional before attempting any techniques outlined in this book.

By reading this document, the reader agrees that the author cannot be held accountable, under any circumstances, for any losses, whether direct or indirect, incurred as a consequence of using the information provided in this document, including but not limited to errors, omissions, or inaccuracies.

CONTENTS

- **2.** COPYRIGHT.
- **6.** HUMAN BODY.
- **24.** STRUCTURE OF THE HANDS.
- **65.** STRUCTURE OF THE LEGS.
- **98.** THANK YOU.

LET'S GO
DRAWINGS

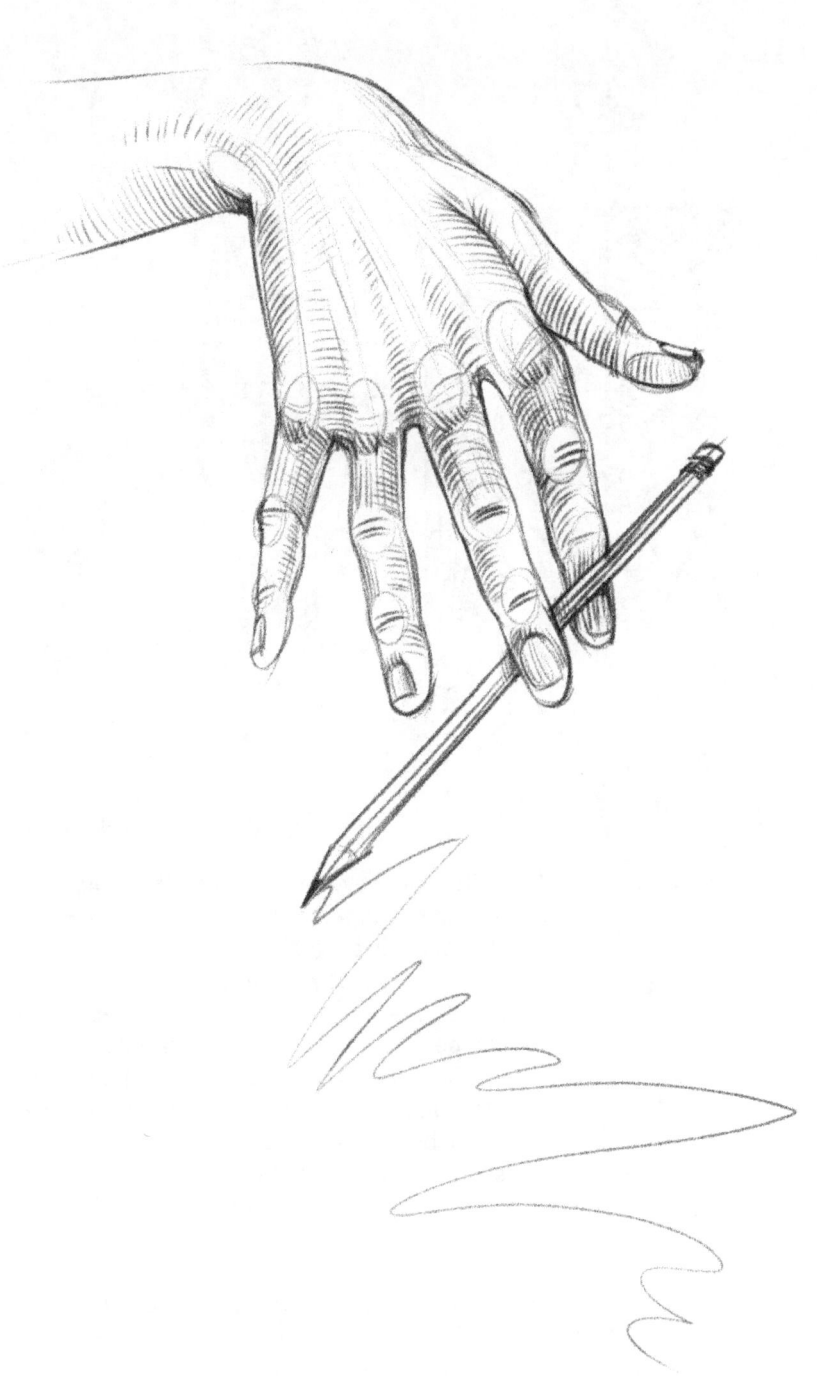

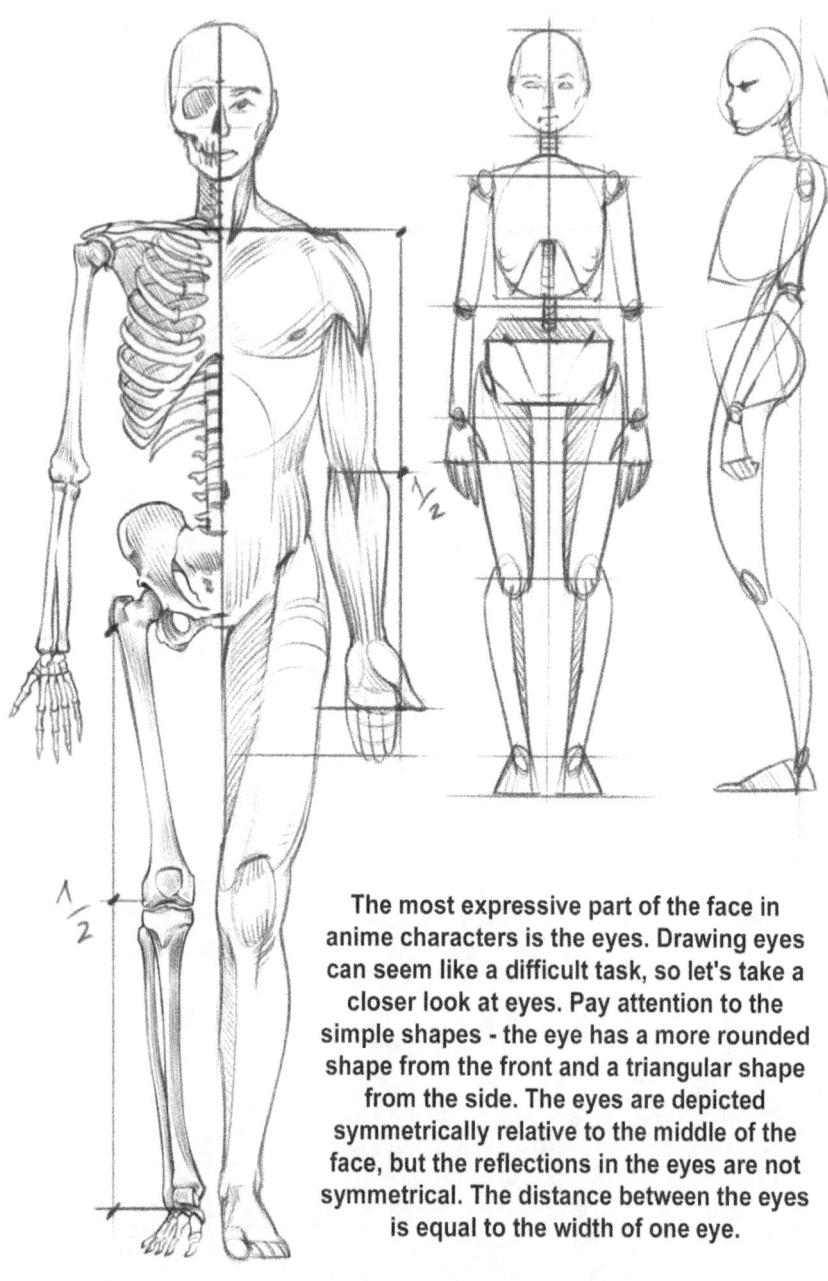

The most expressive part of the face in anime characters is the eyes. Drawing eyes can seem like a difficult task, so let's take a closer look at eyes. Pay attention to the simple shapes - the eye has a more rounded shape from the front and a triangular shape from the side. The eyes are depicted symmetrically relative to the middle of the face, but the reflections in the eyes are not symmetrical. The distance between the eyes is equal to the width of one eye.

However, these proportions may vary depending on the individual characteristics of a person, his posture, and age. For example, children have longer arms and legs relative to the body than adults.

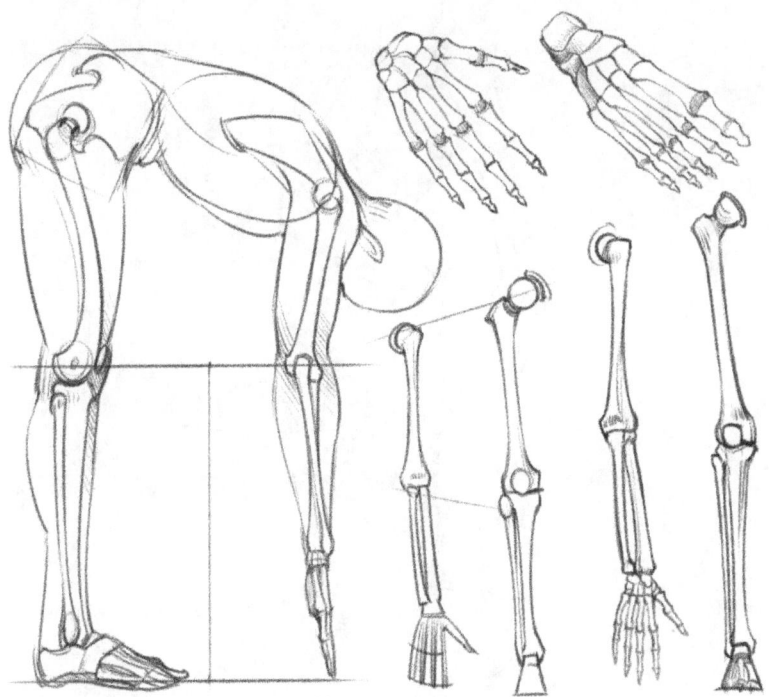

Hands and feet have a lot in common in structure and proportions. Both limbs consist of three parts: the shoulder or thigh (the upper part of the arm or leg), the forearm or lower leg (the middle part), and the hand or foot (the lower part).

If you look at a person's hands and feet, you can see that they have similar proportions. For example, the length of the shoulder is usually about half the length of the arm, and the length of the thigh is about half the length of the leg.

Arms and legs also have many similar bones. For example, the shoulder consists of the scapula and humerus, and the hip consists of the hip joint and femur. The forearm consists of the radius and ulna, and the lower leg consists of the fibula and tibia. The bones of the hand and foot also have a lot in common in structure, such as features of the phalanges or joints and ligaments.

Despite the similarities, there are also some differences between hands and feet. For example, the arms have a more slender and curved appearance than the legs. This is due to the fact that the hands are designed to perform more subtle and precise movements.

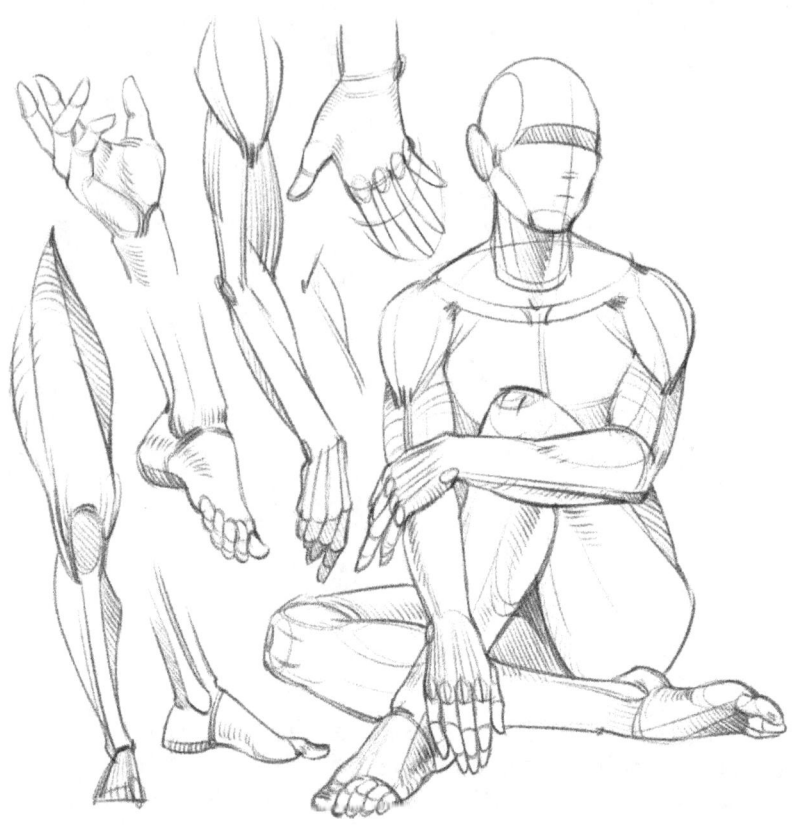

When drawing the human body, it is important for the artist to take into account its proportions and structure. For this, you can use imaginary lines that help you see the main structural elements of the body. Knowing the bone and muscle structure of the body, we know the lines of demarcation of muscles, the key points of the bones, the possible movement of the limbs with the help of joints, etc.

In addition, the human body can be compared to some geometric shapes. For example, the human head is like a sphere, the thigh is like a cylinder, and the lower legs are like cones. These are simple forms that are familiar to us from childhood and will help us better perceive the volume. Different parts of the body have different shapes - more rounded muscular and fatty forms, sharper bony ones.

Similarity to geometric shapes also helps the artist to correctly distribute light and shadow and correctly depict body parts in perspective.

Knowledge of imaginary lines and geometric shapes in drawing the human body is a powerful tool that can help the artist in drawing the human body.

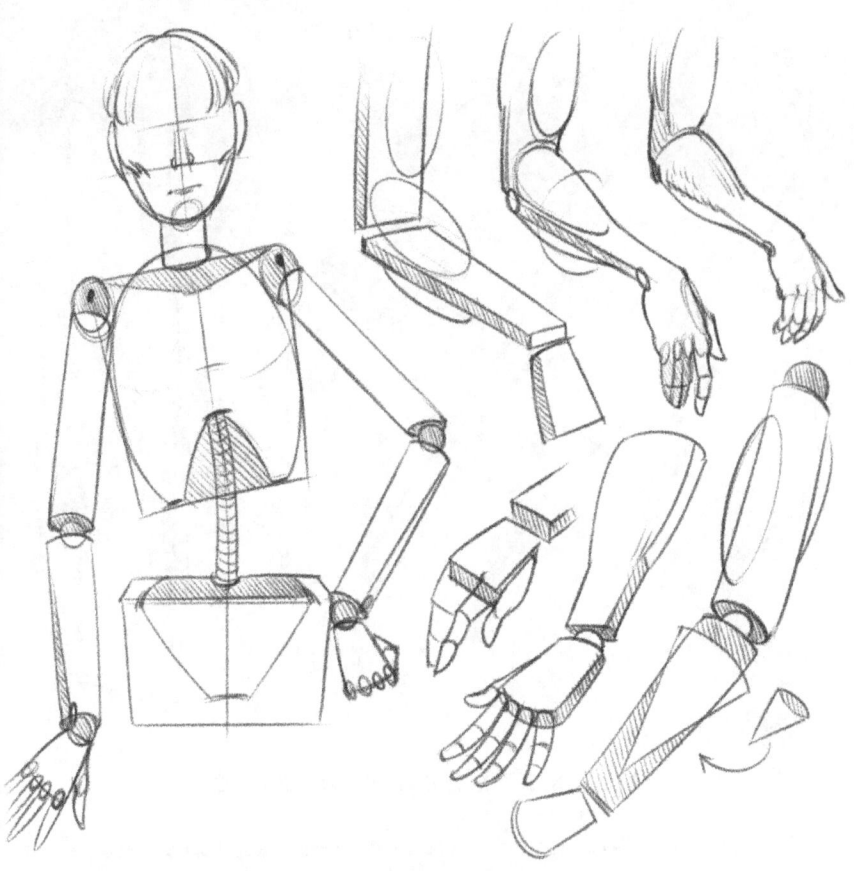

Simplifying body parts to geometric shapes provides a great understanding of human body shapes for the artist. Usually, the upper limbs are depicted in the form of two cylinders, and the brush is a flat rectangular shape. The connection between them can be shown by hinges, which indicate the joints. Most elements can be divided into cylindrical and flat rectangular. Muscle groups can be transferred in egg-shaped forms.

The simplified form of the shoulder can be given in the form of two parts. The cylinder seems to be divided in half and has an egg-shaped biceps in front and triceps in the back.

The forearm in the form of three - the ulnar-radial muscle conditionally separates the extensors and flexors, which are placed in parallel. The forearm tapers to the hand, so it can be depicted as a cone. Visually, the wrist has a flat shape, so it is depicted as a flat parallelepiped at the end of the forearm. The brush can be depicted in the same form. Fingers can be represented by three cylinders (3 phalanges).

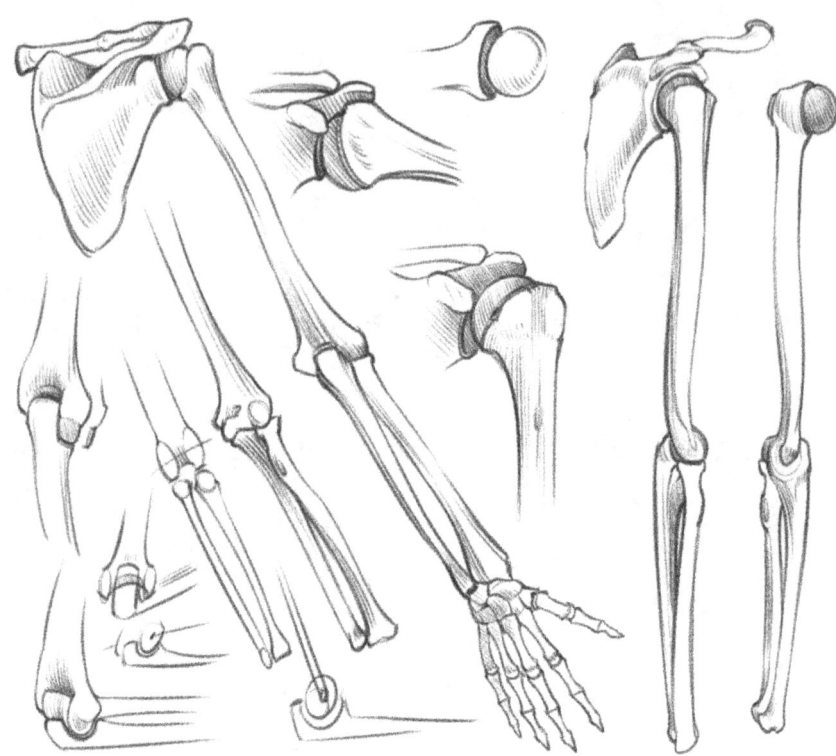

ARM BONES CAN BE DIVIDED INTO GROUPS:

The shoulder girdle consists of the scapula and clavicle. The scapula is a flat bone located in the back of the body. The clavicle is a long, thin bone that connects the shoulder blade to the sternum.

The shoulder consists of the humerus, a long, tubular bone that connects the shoulder girdle to the forearm.

The forearm consists of the radius (a long, thin bone located on the outside of the forearm) and the ulna (a long, thick bone located on the inside of the forearm).

Brush - deserves special attention (next page).

Also, human hands have many joints that ensure their mobility. A stable shoulder joint (hinge) connects the humerus with the scapula. This joint allows the arm to move forward, backward, up, and down. The elbow connects the humerus with the forearm. This joint allows the arm to bend and extend. The radius-ulnar joint connects the radius and ulna. This joint allows the arm to turn in and out.

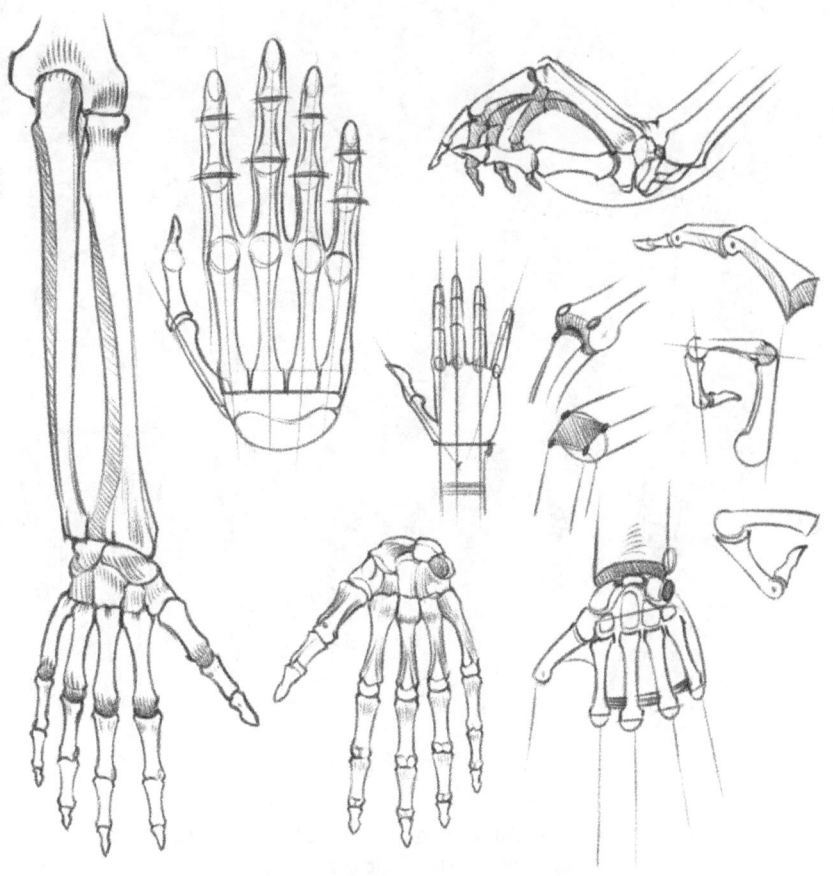

THE HAND CONSISTS OF THE WRIST, FIVE METATARSAL BONES, AND 14 PHALANGES.

The wrist is a part of the hand, which consists of 8 bones arranged in two rows. The bones of the wrist are located at the base of the hand and provide it with stability. The metacarpals are five tubular bones located between the wrists and fingers. They end in a bent or arched shape and give rise to fingers. The bones of the wrist are located in the middle part of the hand and provide it with mobility.

The phalanges of the fingers are the bones that make up the fingers. They can be depicted as cylinders. Each finger has three phalanges: the main, intermediate, and nail. The thumb is different from the other fingers and starts on the inside of the wrist. side of the hand It is also shown with 3 cylinders, but only has 2 phalanges. The main first cylinder is the carpal bone, which is more mobile and different from the others.

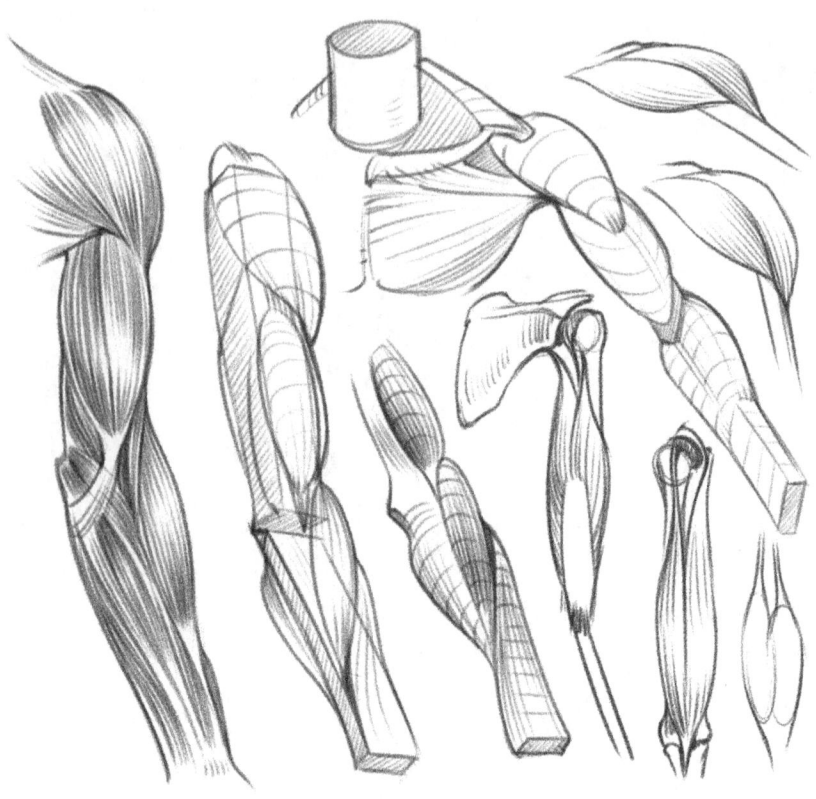

Let's consider the muscular structure of the hands and their simplified scheme. Arm muscles can be divided into several groups.

The shoulder girdle muscle is a deltoid muscle that covers the entire front and side of the shoulder. You can use a ball to draw the deltoid muscle. The ball can help the artist determine the general shape of the shoulder and the location of the deltoid muscle.

Shoulder muscles - biceps and triceps. The biceps are located on the front of the shoulder and are responsible for bending the arm at the elbow joint. When the arm is folded forward, the biceps are strongly highlighted and take on a more rounded shape. At the end of the arm, there is a small indentation, which is related to the volume of the biceps and the shape of the brachioradialis. The triceps is located on the back of the shoulder and is responsible for extending the arm at the elbow joint. It is more pronounced when the arm is bent, and less pronounced when the arm is straightened. It can be simplified to an oval shape divided in half.

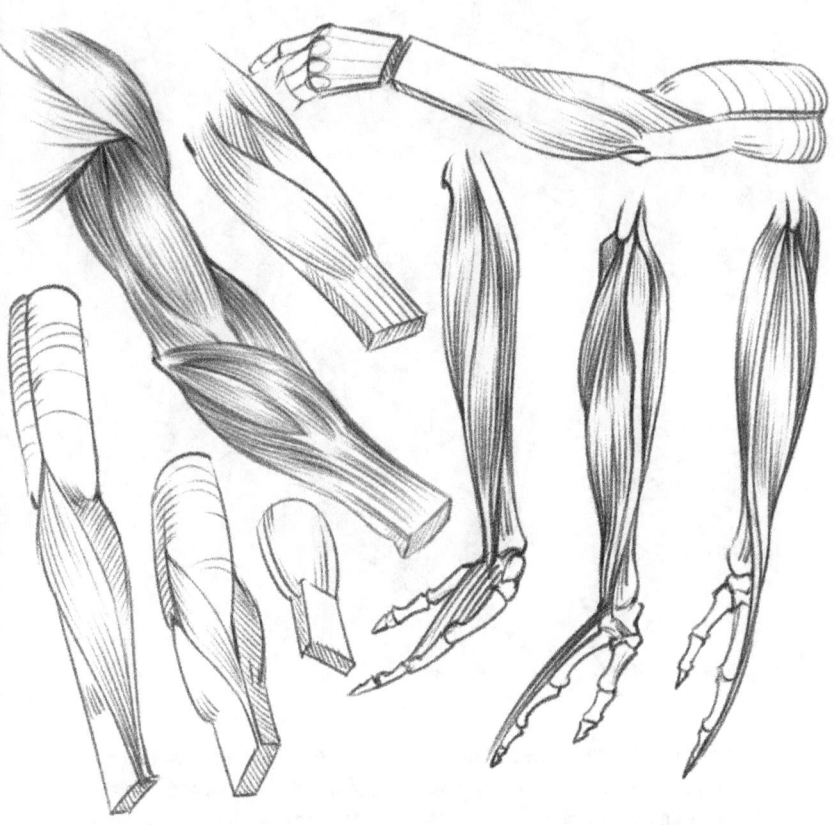

The forearm is often depicted as a cylinder or cone because it has a larger muscle volume on top and tapers to the wrist. At the bottom, the forearm has a flatter shape, especially when the hand is at rest or turned palm up.

The muscles of the forearm provide movement of the radius and ulna. They are divided into three groups. The brachioradialis group starts at the top of the arm and ends at the wrist on the side of the thumb. It separates the flexors and extensors on the inside of the arm. The extensors begin at the elbow and attach to the back of the arm. Parallel to the extensors are the flexors, which are located on the inside and are attached to the palm.

Practice drawing the main muscles of the hand using simple shapes. The more you draw, the better you will understand the structure of the hands and be able to create more realistic drawings.

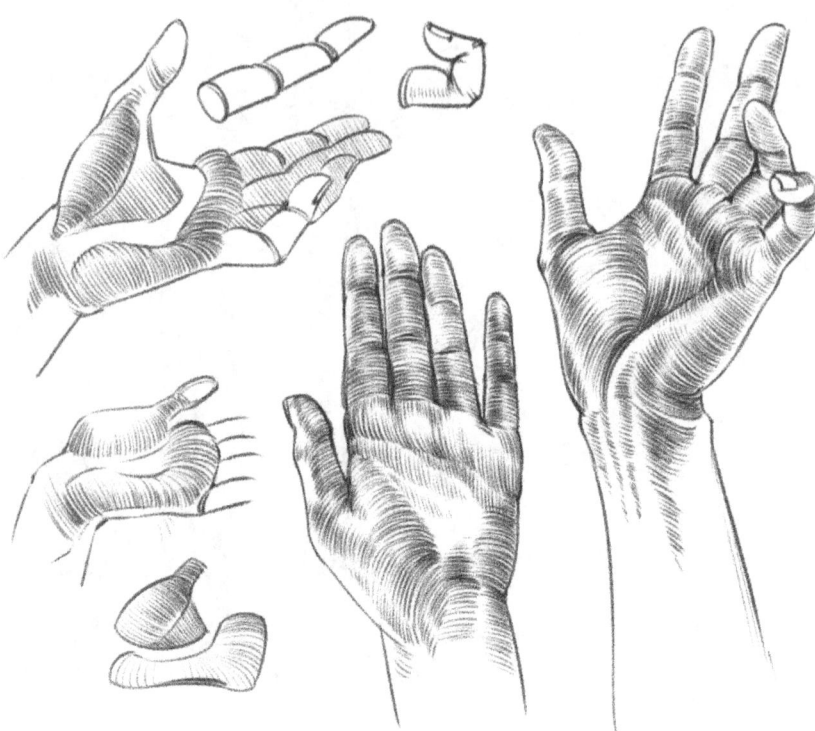

Volumetric masses are located on the palm of a person - these are muscles (muscle pads), fatty tissues, and tendons. They provide movement of fingers and hands, better contact with the surface to which we touch, soften impacts, and provide thermal insulation.

These masses also determine the volume and contours of the palm. The shape and position of the muscular volume masses on the palm can change depending on the position of the hand and the way we use our fingers. For example, when we clench our fingers into a fist, the muscular volumetric masses on the palm become more noticeable.

The masses stand out the most near the beginning of the fingers. They are created from the bending of the fingers for better holding of objects and support, the base of the thumb is especially voluminous, which can be directed towards the other fingers and cover the object. There is also a noticeable change in the schematic image of the phalanges, which have become more rounded than cylindrical.

Volumetric masses on the palm have different shapes and sizes depending on the person. They can be bigger or smaller, soft or hard.

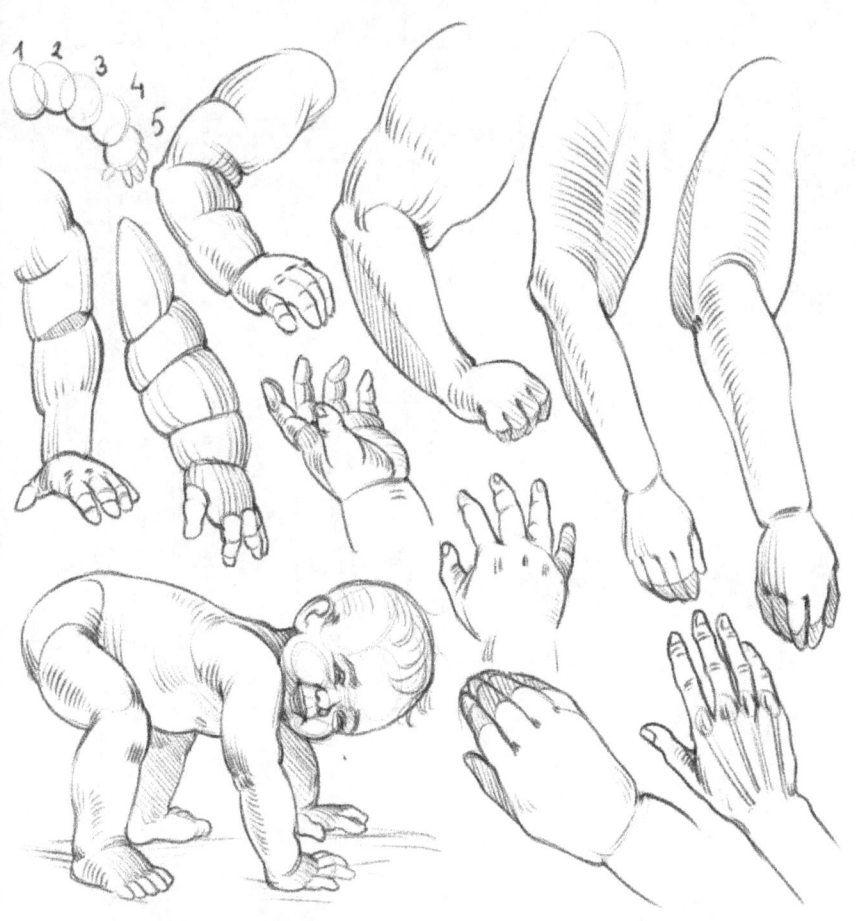

The hands of fat people and children have several features in common. Obese people have more muscle and fat than people of normal weight. This means that the hands of fat people will be larger and rounder. In addition, the hands of fat people may have less pronounced veins and tendons. This is due to the fact that these people have thicker skin than people of normal weight. The location of the main muscles and bones remains unchanged, but the volumetric masses are larger and less elastic.

To make the hands appear more voluminous, it is important to use darker shadows to create a sense of volume and depth in the folds of the skin.

Children's hands are different from adults' hands. They are, as a rule, thinner and more delicate, with less developed muscles that form volumetric folds (4 folds along the entire length of the arm). Also, children's hands are larger in relation to the proportions of the body and are more rounded.

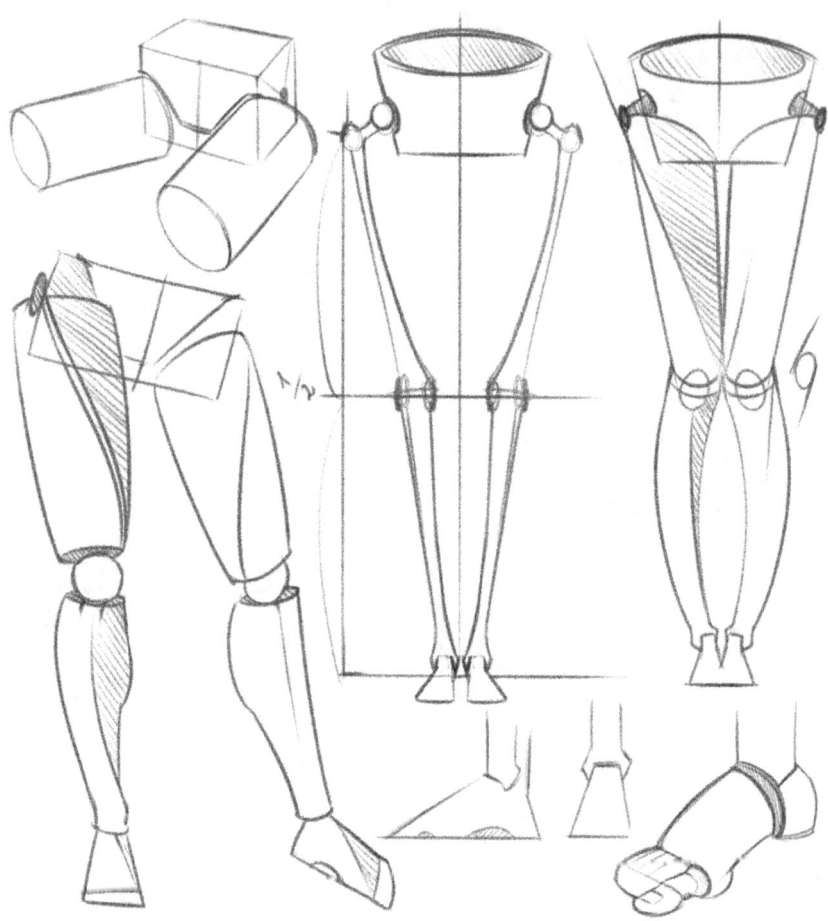

Legs, like hands, can be divided into 3 parts: thigh, lower leg and foot. The knee is a complex joint that connects the thigh and lower leg and divides the leg into 2 equal parts.

The thigh is the widest part of the leg. It is located between the pelvis and the knee joint. The thigh can be depicted as a cylinder, which can take a conical shape, tapering to the knee. Most often, we draw diagonal lines corresponding to the bone and muscle structure of the legs, which help to depict the limbs from different sides.

From the knee to the ankle is the shin, which has the shape of an elongated cone. The shape resembles a forearm: fleshy muscle forms above and tendons below the ankle.

The shin connects to the foot from below. Its shape resembles a wedge, which has an arched curve from below. This provides stability and balance.

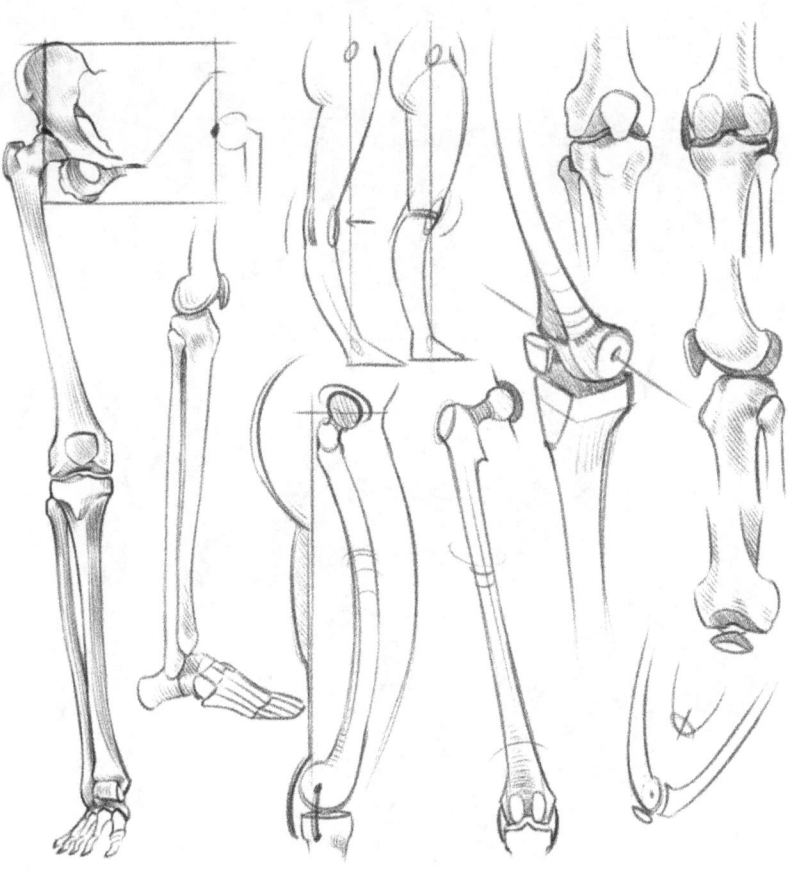

To understand the shape of the legs, it is worth considering the structure of the bones of the legs.

The femur is the longest bone in the human body. It is a long tubular bone that is located in the femoral part of the leg. It is connected to the pelvis by the hip (hip) joint. The hip joint is a hinge joint that allows the hip to rotate in different directions.

The tibia (big and small) are two bones that are located in the lower part of the leg. They are connected to each other by the joint and the knee joint with the femur.

The knee joint allows the legs to bend and extend, that is, to move back and forth, to the point of alignment of the leg. You can bend only along an imaginary axis, it is impossible to do it sideways.

Ankle joint - connects the leg to the foot. This joint resembles a groove, but this joint is more flexible than the knee.

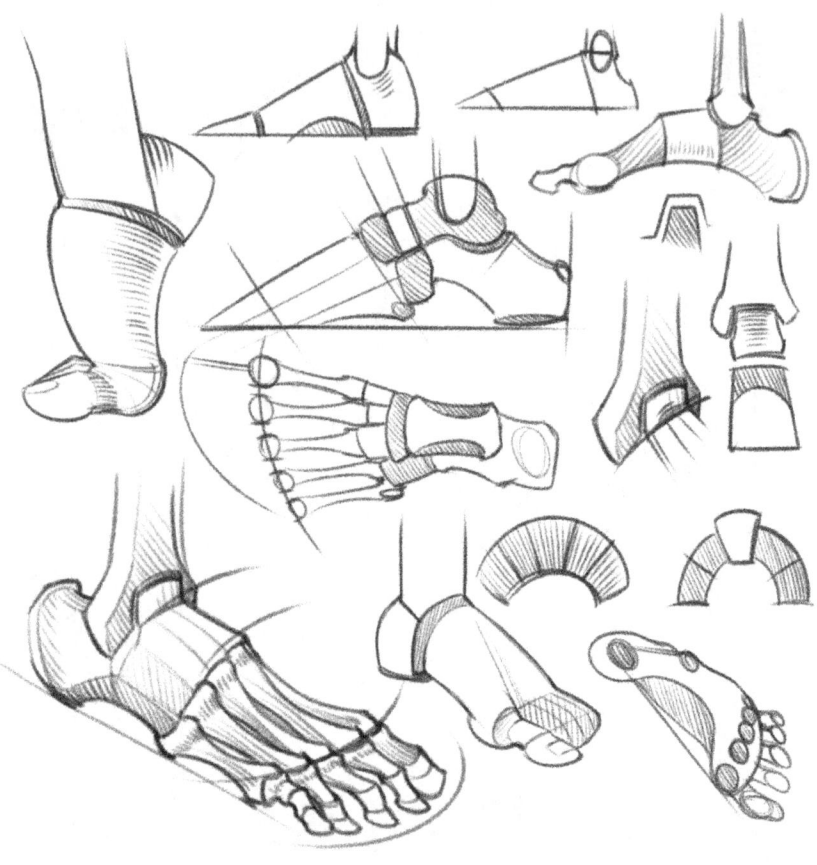

The foot is divided into three sections. It has a curve in the form of an arc in the middle part of the foot, a massive shape (heel) in the back part of the foot, and a wedge-shaped narrowing in the front part - the toes.

The rear part of the foot is the support of the foot. The calcaneus is the largest bone of the foot and acts as a shock absorber when walking and running. The talus is located between the calcaneus and the tibia. It helps to stabilize the ankle joint and connects the heel bone with the midfoot bones.

The middle part of the foot consists of wedge-shaped bones, to which the tendons of the foot muscles are attached, which provide movement of the toes. Three wedge-shaped bones are connected by joints and form the arch of the foot. The fourth and fifth sphenoid bones help stabilize the foot.

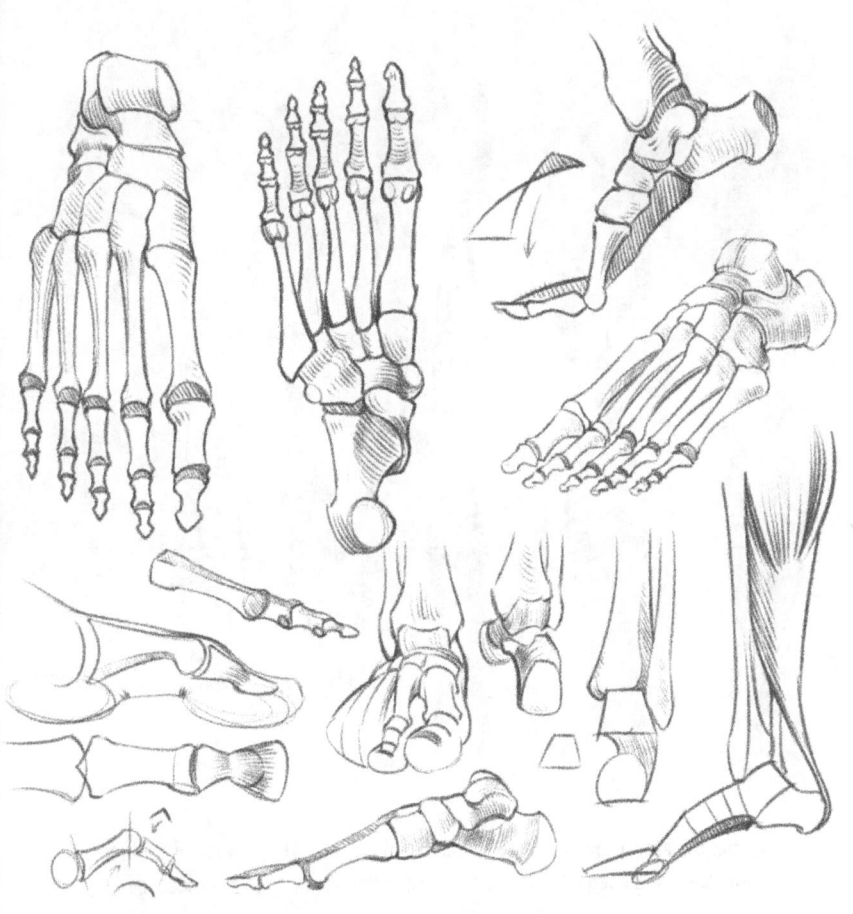

The front part of the foot is formed by the phalanges of the fingers - this is a group of 14 bones that are connected to each other by joints. Like fingers, the big toe has two phalanges, the other fingers have three. There is a nail on the last phalanx. Also, each finger has its own metatarsal bone (metatarsal bones - 5 long tubular bones that connect the phalanges of the fingers and the middle of the foot and ensure their mobility).

The phalanges of the fingers have 2 main types of joints: the sphere at the base of the metatarsal bones (as in the hand at the end of the fist) and the pulley between the phalanges for flexion-extension.

The same types of joints are united by the talus, the pulley for flexion-extension, and the sphere for turning the foot.

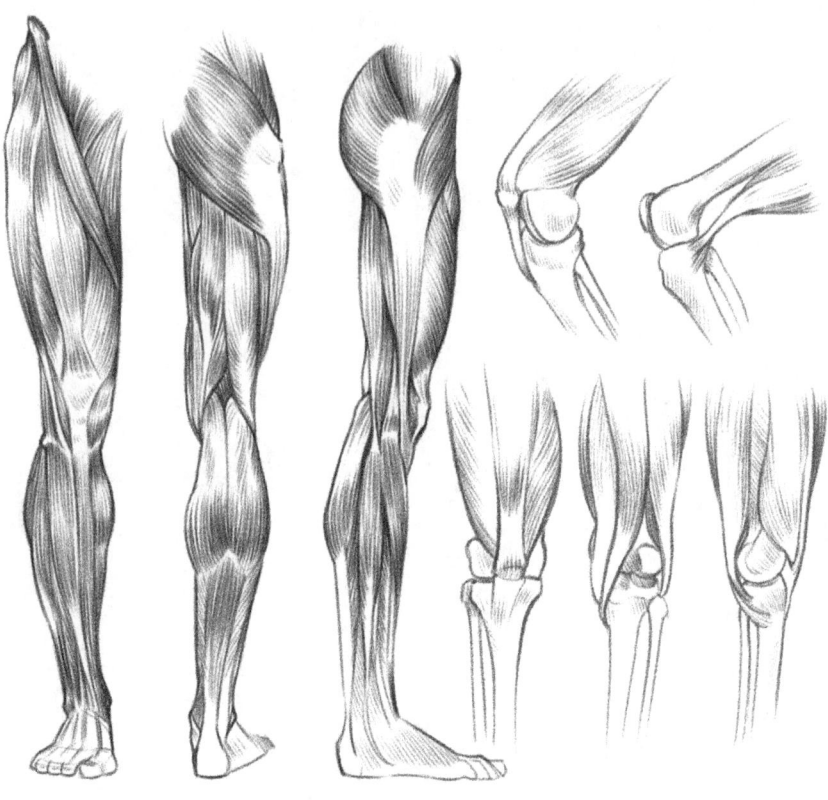

Leg muscles are a group of muscles located in the legs. They are responsible for the movement of the legs, as well as for maintaining the body in a vertical position.

Pay attention to the bend of the leg. The leg in the thigh has more volume in the front due to the massive quadriceps, and the rounded calf muscle is located on the back of the lower leg. This contributes to the fact that the thigh goes forward and the lower leg back.

Consider the main muscles of the thigh. The gluteus maximus is the largest muscle in the human body. It is located in the back of the thigh and is responsible for extending the hip and turning the hip to the side. The quadriceps femoris in the front of the thigh and the hamstring in the back of the thigh are responsible for bending the hip and turning the hip to the side.

The main muscles of the thigh are attached to the knee (shown in detail in the illustrations) and provide stability and mobility of the knee joint.

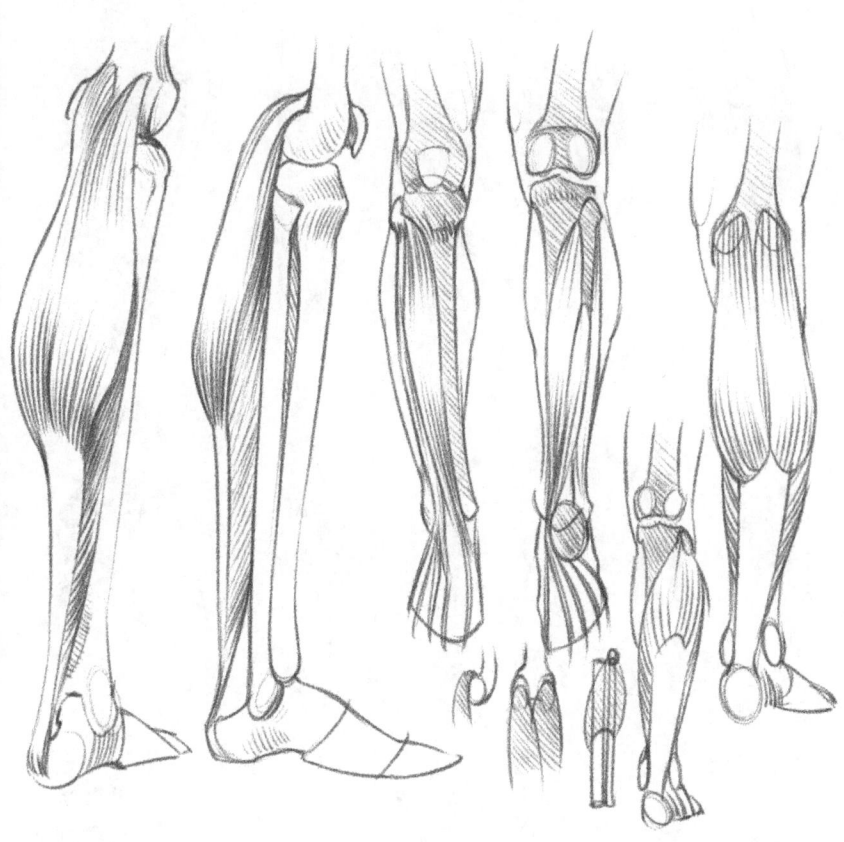

The calf muscles are located in the lower leg. They are responsible for bending and extending the lower leg, as well as for turning the foot in different directions. The triceps muscle of the leg (triceps surae) is a group of three muscles that are located in the back of the leg. They are responsible for bending the lower leg and turning the foot (the calf muscle bends the leg at the knee joint). The front tibial muscle (tibialis anterior) is located in the front part of the lower leg. It is responsible for extending the lower leg and turning the foot to the side. The posterior fibular muscle (longus flexor digitorum) is located on the back of the lower leg. It is responsible for bending the toes.

The most noticeable muscle is the triceps, especially when the leg is under tension. It is divided into the biceps calf muscle (which resembles the triceps muscle of the hand) and the soleus muscle. They connect and together form a common tendon that attaches to the heel.

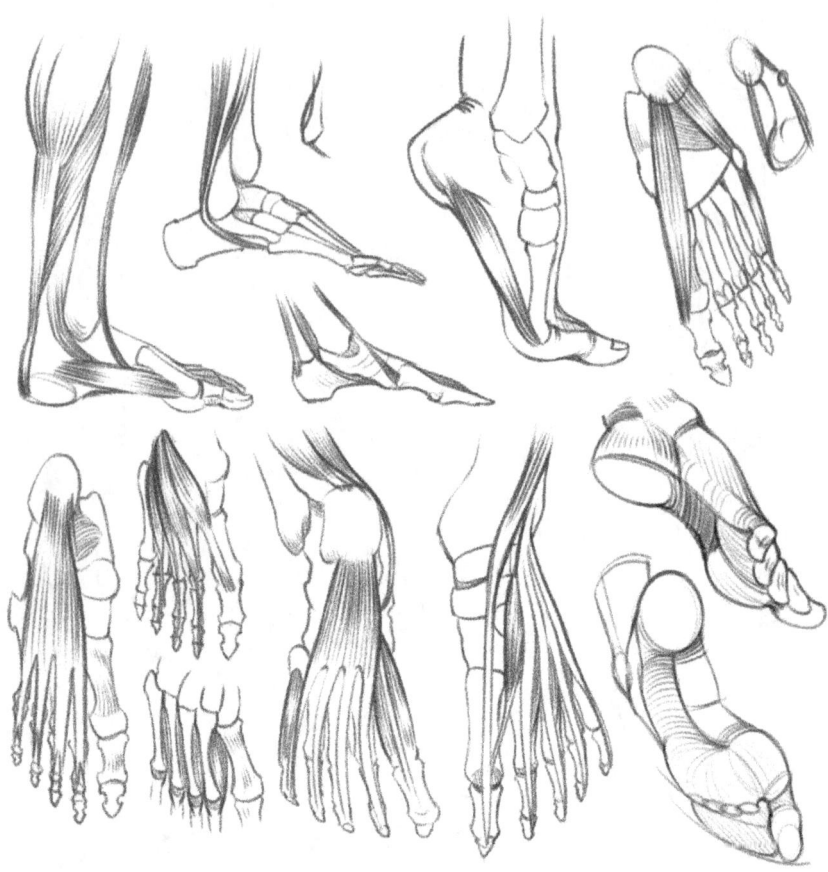

The muscles of the foot are located in the foot. They are responsible for the movement of the toes, as well as for maintaining the foot in the correct position.

The main muscles of the foot, which are important for an artist to know:

Interosseous muscles are a group of muscles that are located between the bones of the foot. They are responsible for the movement of the toes.

The toe flexors are a group of muscles that are located in the back of the foot and are responsible for bending the toes.

The extensor muscles of the toes are a group of muscles that are located in the front of the foot and are responsible for extending the toes.

The top of the foot is solid, while the sole of the foot has muscular and fatty bulks (again similar to the structure of the upper limbs).

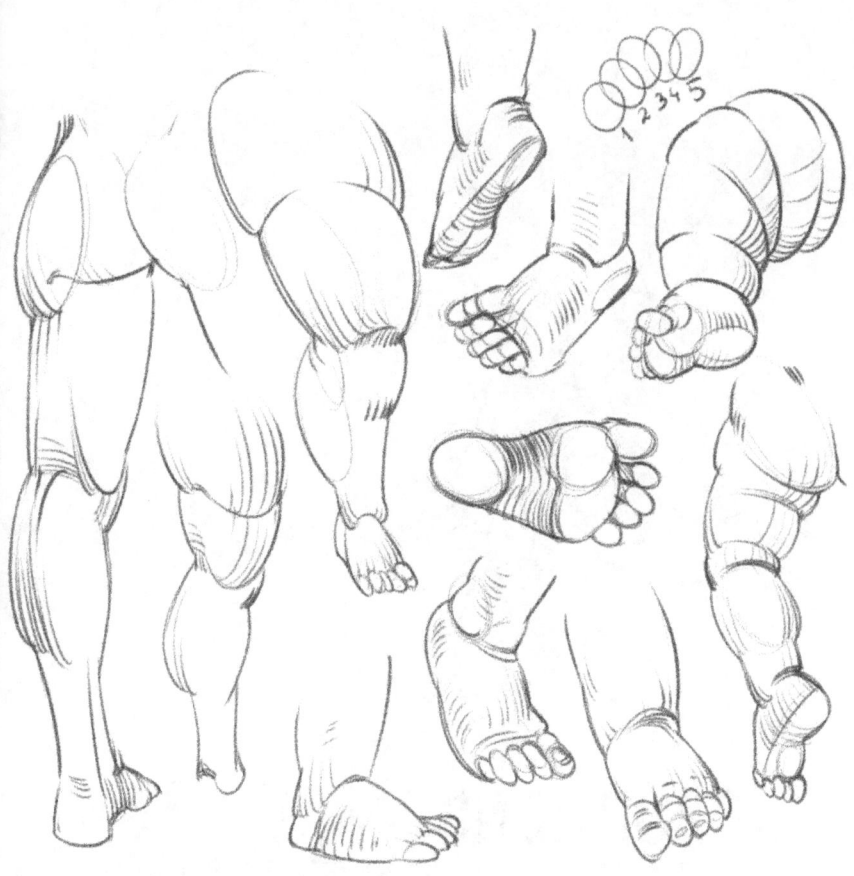

Children's legs have a more rounded structure than the legs of adults. This is due to the fact that children's muscles are not yet fully formed. In addition, children's bones have not yet fully strengthened. They are more elastic and flexible than adults.

To convey the rounded shape of children's legs, artists often use simple shapes. For example, the thigh can be depicted in the form of a sphere, the leg - in the form of a cylinder, and the foot - in the form of a trapezoid. Or a set of spheres that repeat the fold lines.

The legs of fat people also have a more rounded structure. This is due to the fact that fat people have a layer of subcutaneous fat. Fat is deposited on all parts of the body, including the legs. In addition, fat people often have muscle hypertrophy (muscles may be less developed than in people of normal weight). It also contributes to a more rounded shape of the legs.

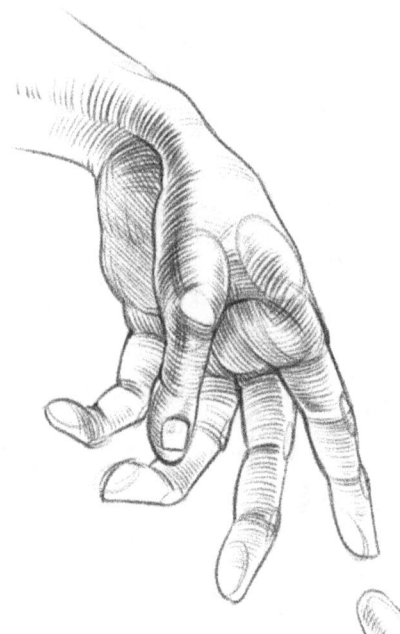

PROPORTIONS OF THE HAND

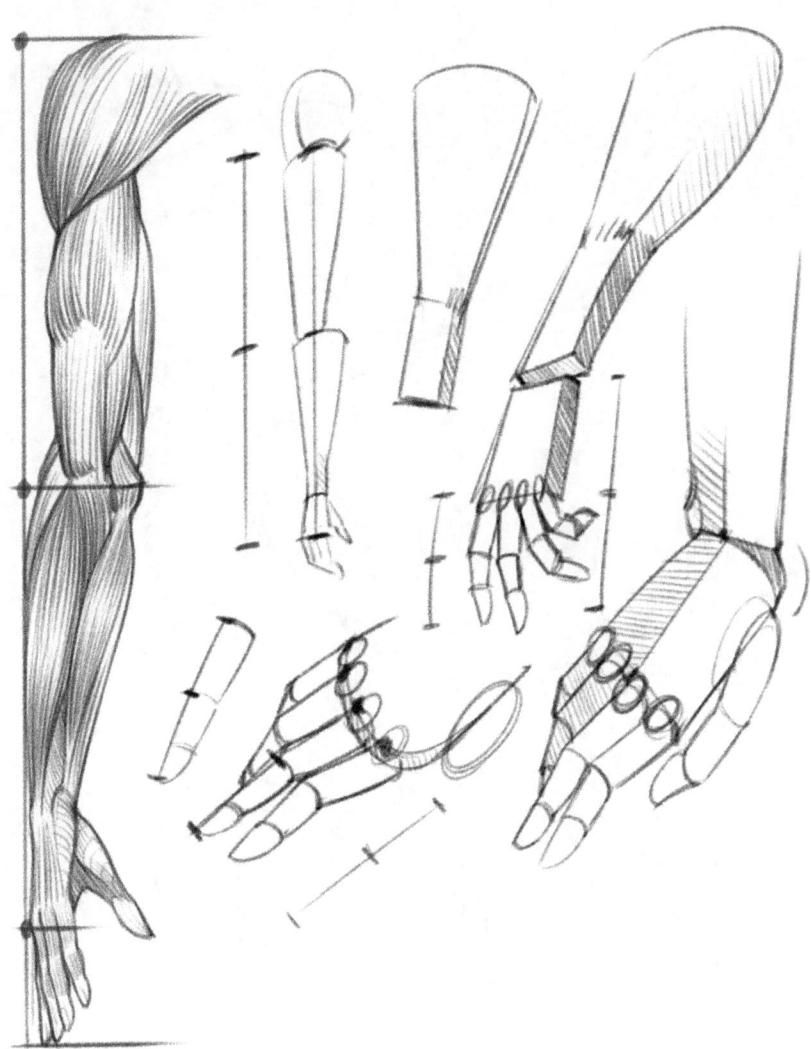

Consider the main proportions of the hands. The elbow joint is located in the middle from the tip of the shoulder to the hand bent into a fist. The length of the longest finger is equal to the length of the body side of the palm and wrist. The length of the first phalanx of the fingers is approximately equal to the length of the next two phalanges.

The shoulder and forearm can be depicted as cylinders narrowed to the bottom, the delta as a sphere. The bottom of the forearm has a larger flat shape, like the palm. The cylinders of the phalanges of the fingers go from the palm.

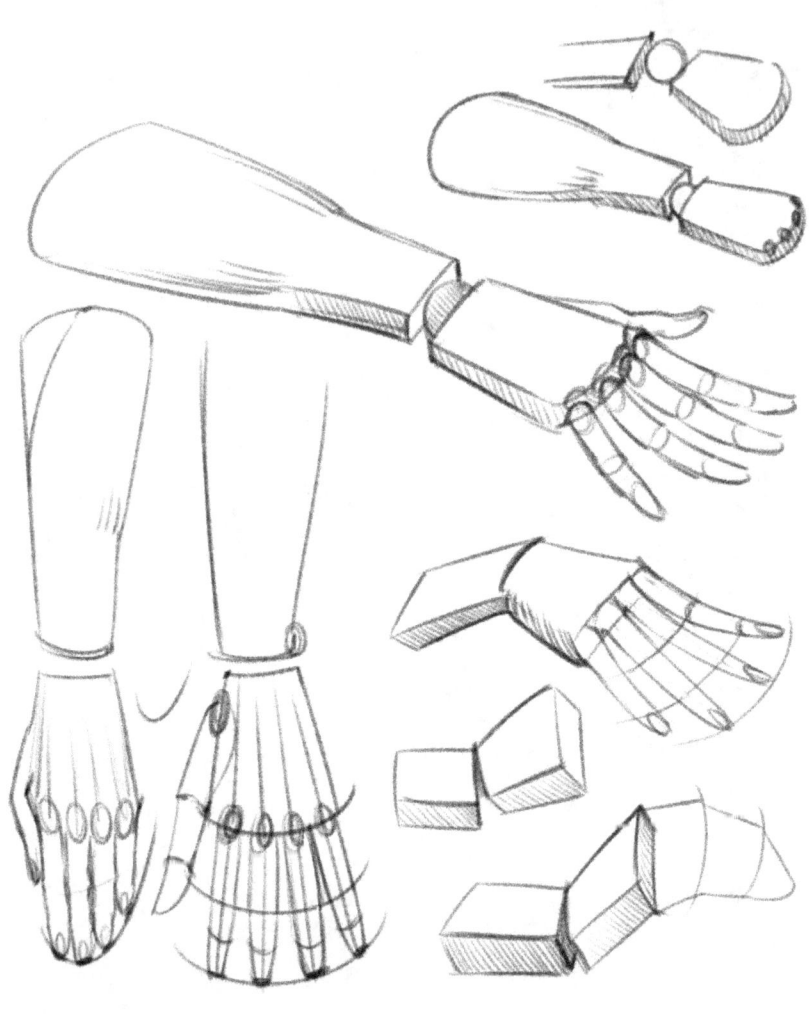

The hand is connected to the forearm by the wrist. Visually, the wrist has a flat shape, so it is depicted as a flat parallelepiped at the end of the forearm. The brush can be depicted in the same form. On the other side of the hand, you should mark the beginning of 4 fingers, the thumb is different and starts from the wrist on the inside of the hand. The fingers begin from the metacarpal bones, which can be represented by three cylinders (3 phalanges). Usually, the beginning of the phalanges is marked with ellipses.

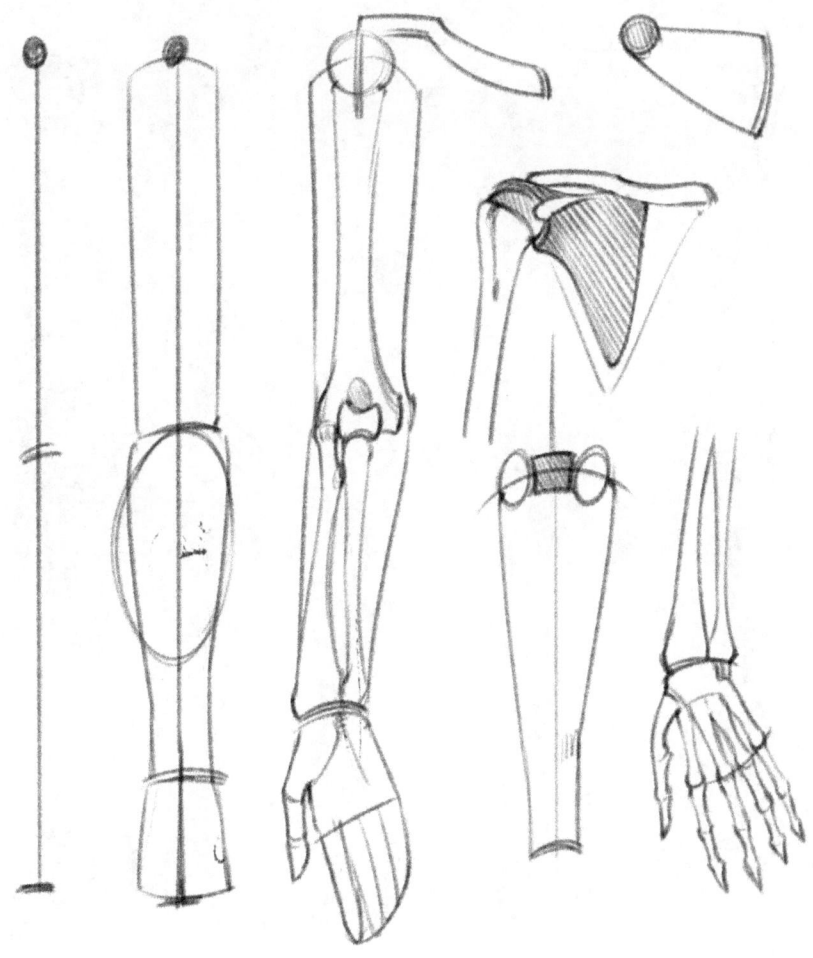

The main joints of the hands are the shoulder, elbow, and wrist.

The shoulder joint (hinge) connects the humerus with the scapula. It allows us to perform shoulder movements such as raising our arms, lowering our arms, turning our arms to the right and left, and rotating.

The elbow joint connects the humerus to the forearm and allows us to bend and extend the arm at the elbow.

The carpal joint connects the forearm to the hand and ensures mobility of the hand and fingers.

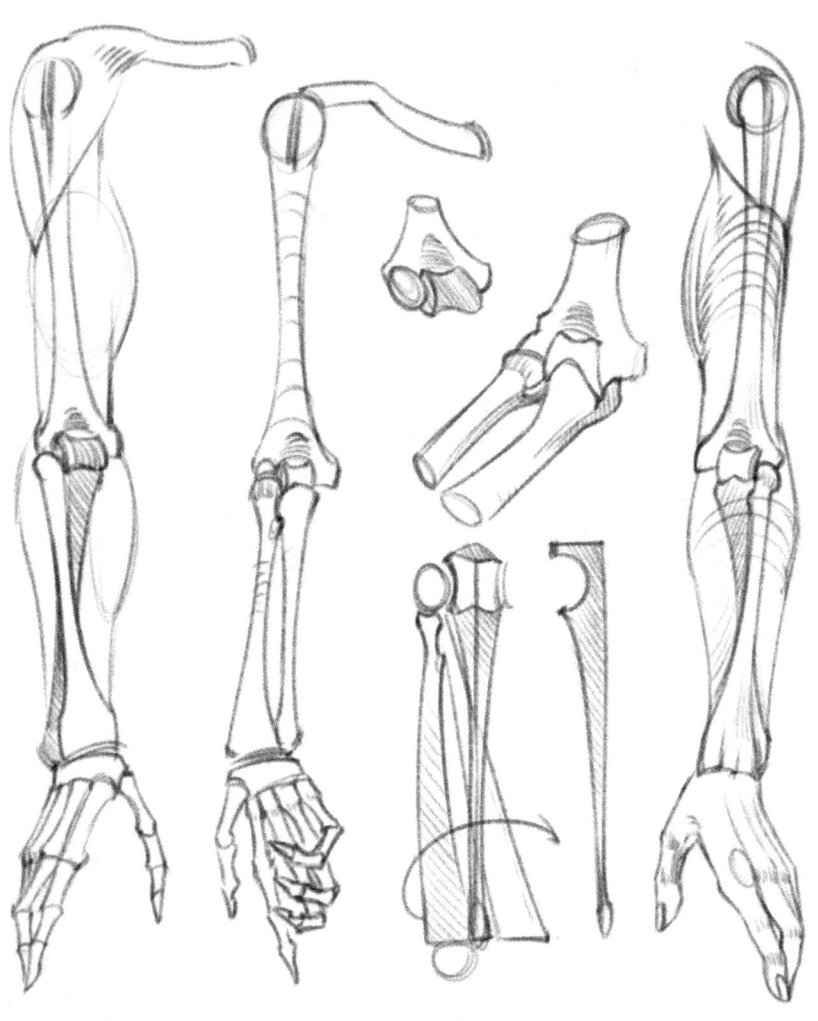

The rotation of the bones of the forearm is called pronation and supronation. During pronation, the radius rotates around its axis so that its lower end moves up and forward, and the upper end - down and back. This causes the palm of the hand to rotate so that its back surface faces down. During supination, the radius rotates around its axis in the opposite direction. This causes the palm of the hand to rotate so that its palm surface faces down.

Pronation and supination occur in the proximal radioulnar joint. This joint connects the radius and ulna of the forearm.

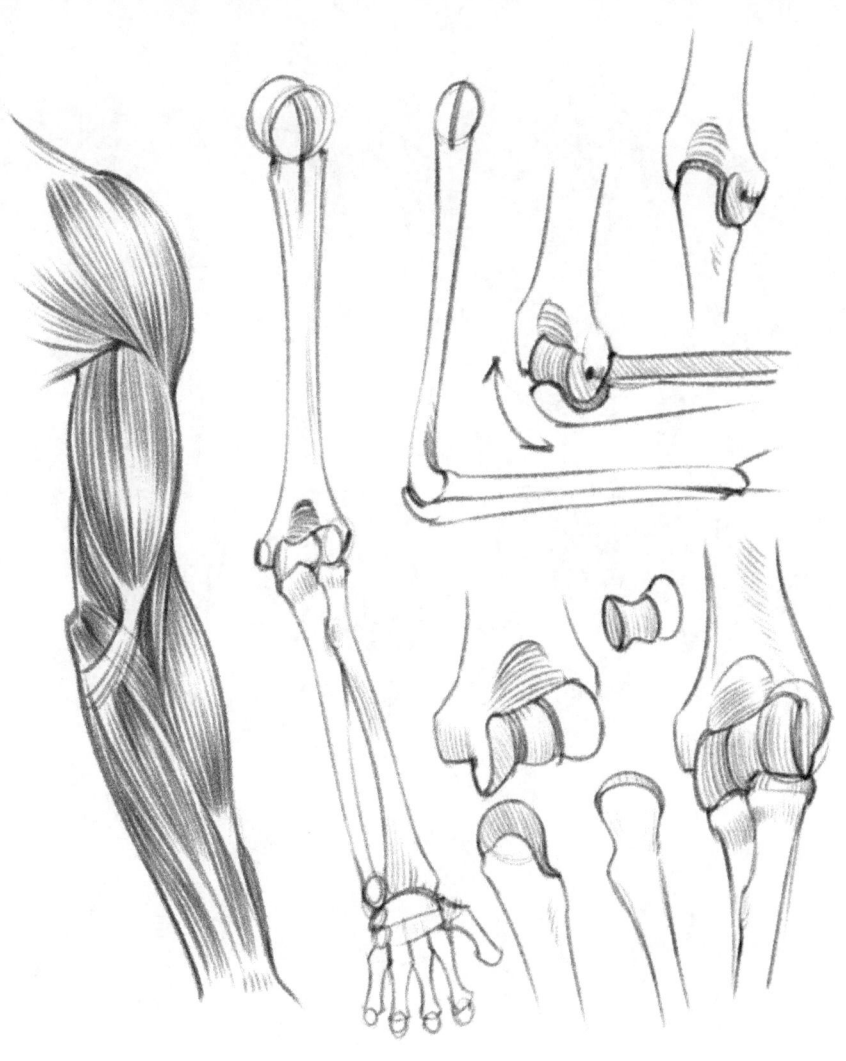

The elbow joint is a complex joint that connects the humerus with the forearm (radius and ulna).

The elbow joint has two axes of rotation, which allows you to perform a wider range of movements than in a single joint. It also has three articular surfaces that are interconnected by ligaments. This provides greater strength and stability of the joint.

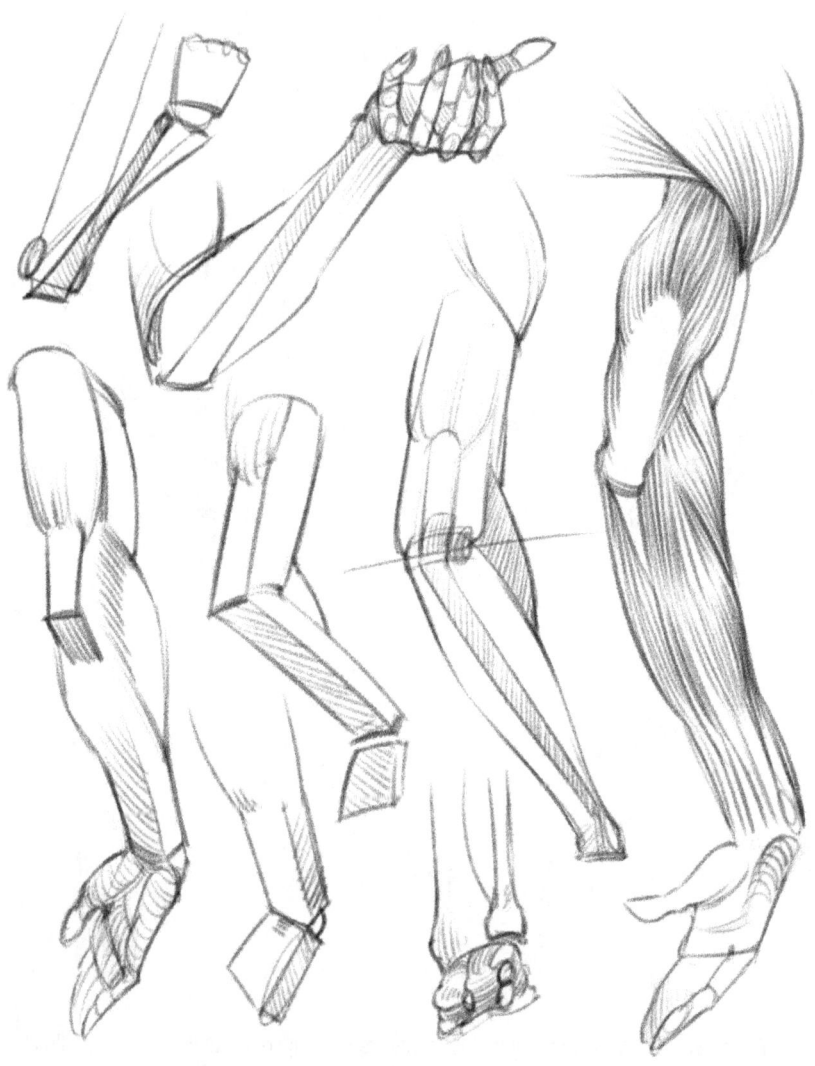

When bending the arm, the elbow takes a sharp shape. It is worth highlighting the ulna - this will help to understand how the bones in the elbow joint move. For example, when the arm is bent at the elbow joint, the front axis of the elbow joint moves forward, while the back axis of the elbow joint remains stationary. This causes the humerus to move closer to the forearm.

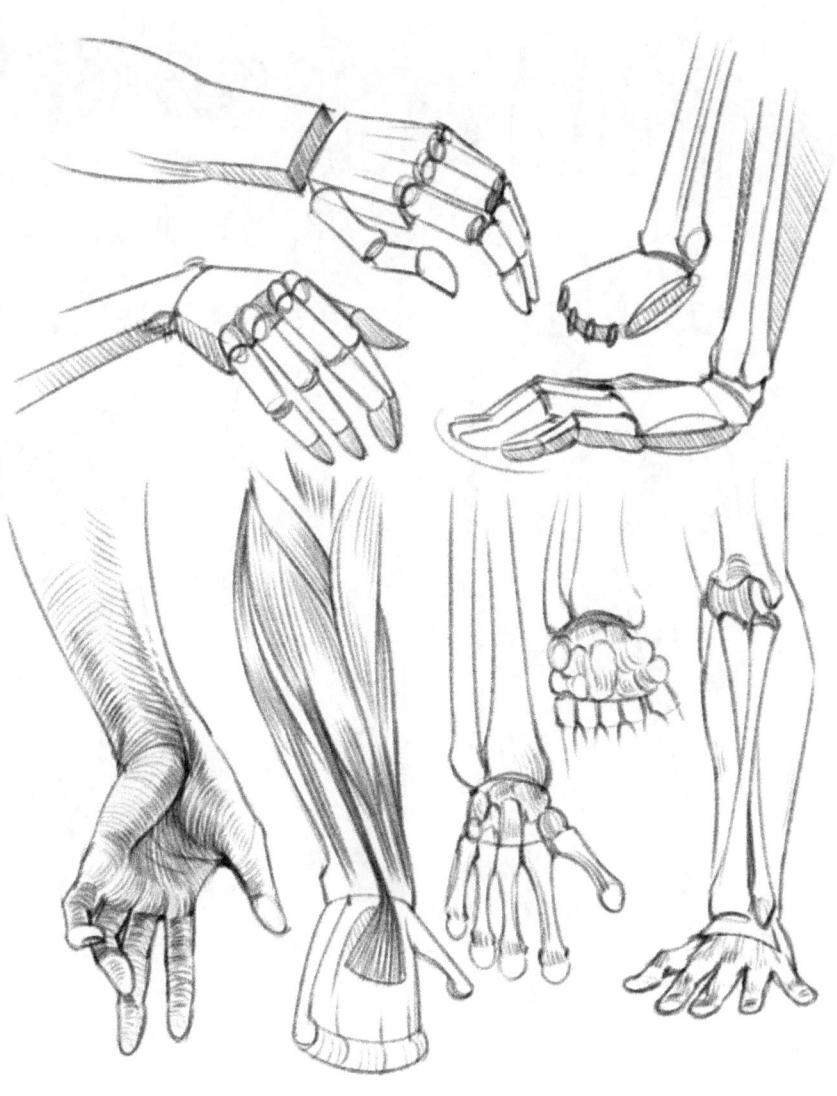

The bottom of the forearm, or the area where the forearm joins the hand, is flatter than the rest of the forearm. This is due to the fact that this part of the forearm is connected to the flat wrist and has a narrowing of muscle forms (tendons) that provide a wide range of movements of the hand.

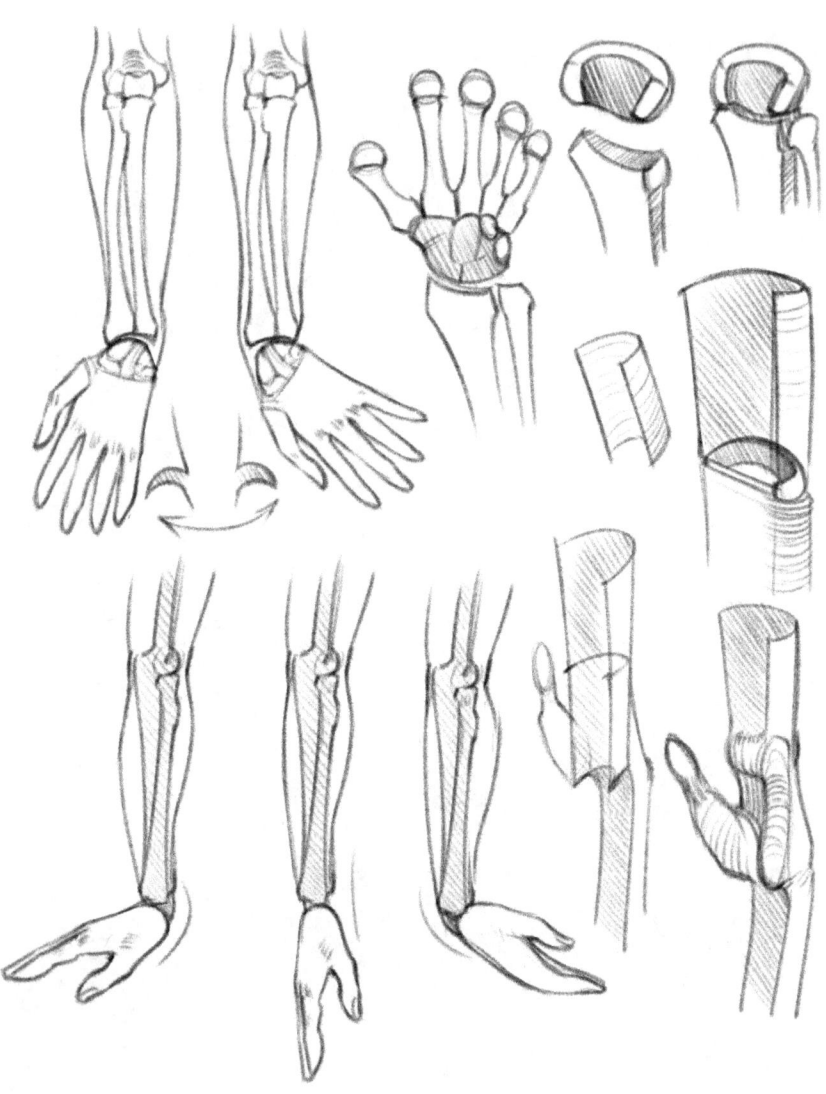

The wrist can be shown with an arched form from the outside. sides and flat from the inside. It can be extended by forming the bend of the palm. This complex structure allows the wrist to perform many movements, such as flexion and extension of the hand, abduction and adduction of the hand, pronation and supination of the hand, flexion and extension of the fingers, abduction and adduction of the fingers.

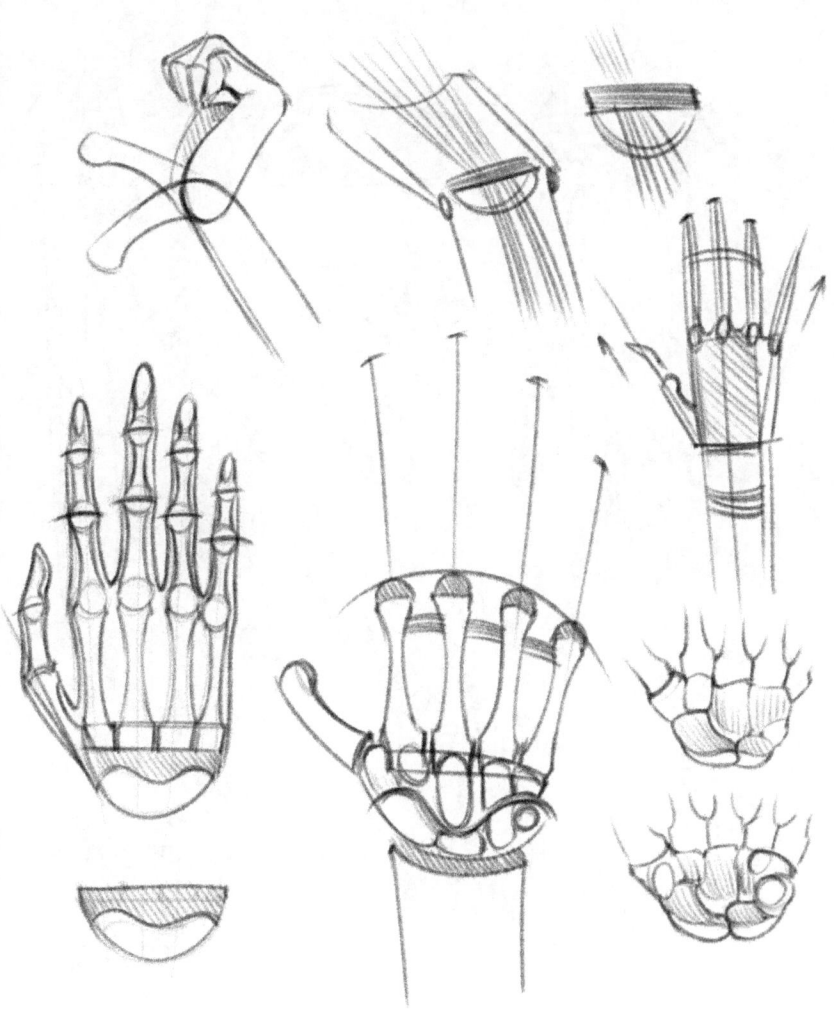

The wrist consists of eight bones connected to each other by ligaments. Despite the flat shape, the wrist allows the hand to move in all directions.

We can simplify the structure of the wrist by dividing it into 2 rows. The proximal row of carpal bones forms an articular surface that articulates with the forearm, and the distal row of carpal bones forms an articular surface that articulates with the hand.

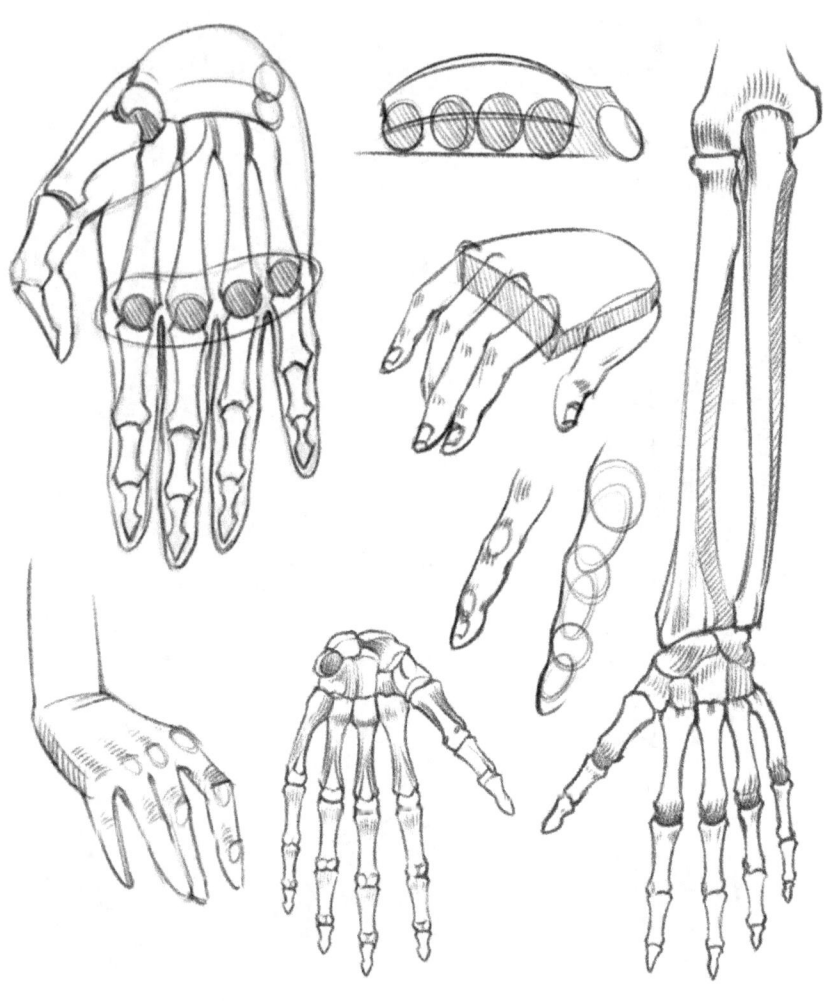

The hand is a mobile part of the upper limb, which consists of the wrist, wrist, and fingers. The metacarpals are five tubular bones located between the wrist and fingers. They end in a bent or arched shape and give rise to fingers. We will mark the beginning of the fingers with ellipses. When the fingers are bent, the ends of the metacarpals and phalanges are clearly visible through the smaller layer of skin on the back side, and we can really see the rounding of the shapes.

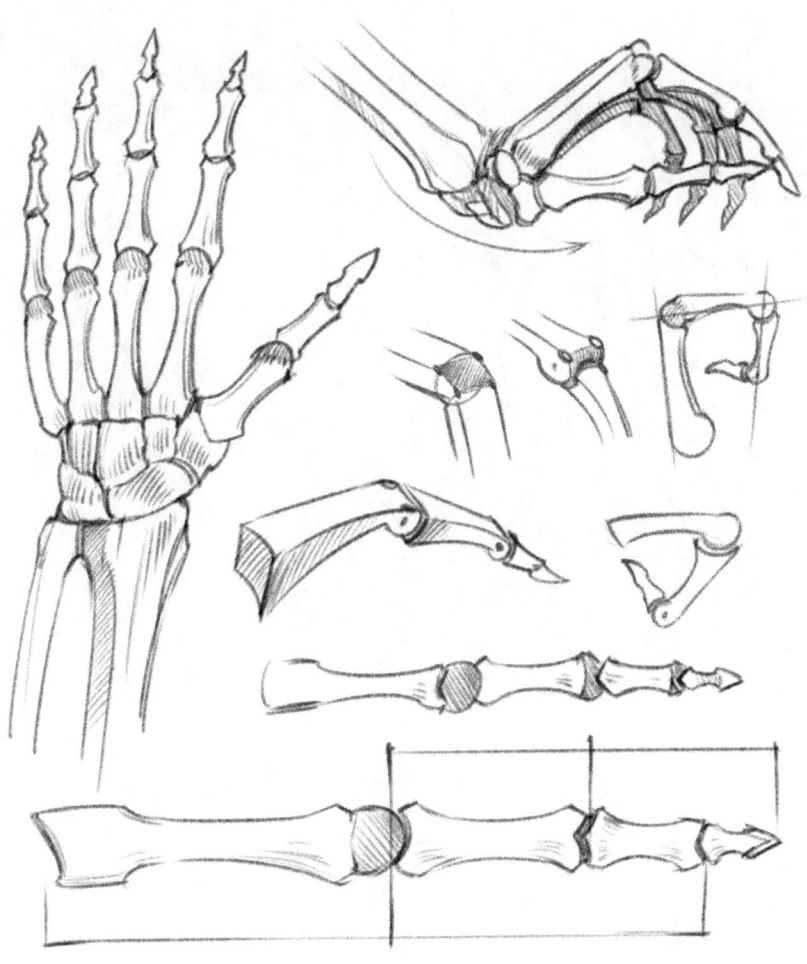

The phalanges of the fingers are the bones that make up the fingers. The length of the longest finger is equal to the length of the metacarpal (the length from the end of the ulna at the wrist to the end of the fist). Each finger, except for the big one, has three phalanges: the main, middle, and nail. The length of the first phalanx is equal to the next two, and the length of the metacarpal bone is equal to the length of the next two phalanges.

Finger phalanges can be simplified to the shape of cylinders. Or give them a more truncated shape, which characterizes the features of the structure.

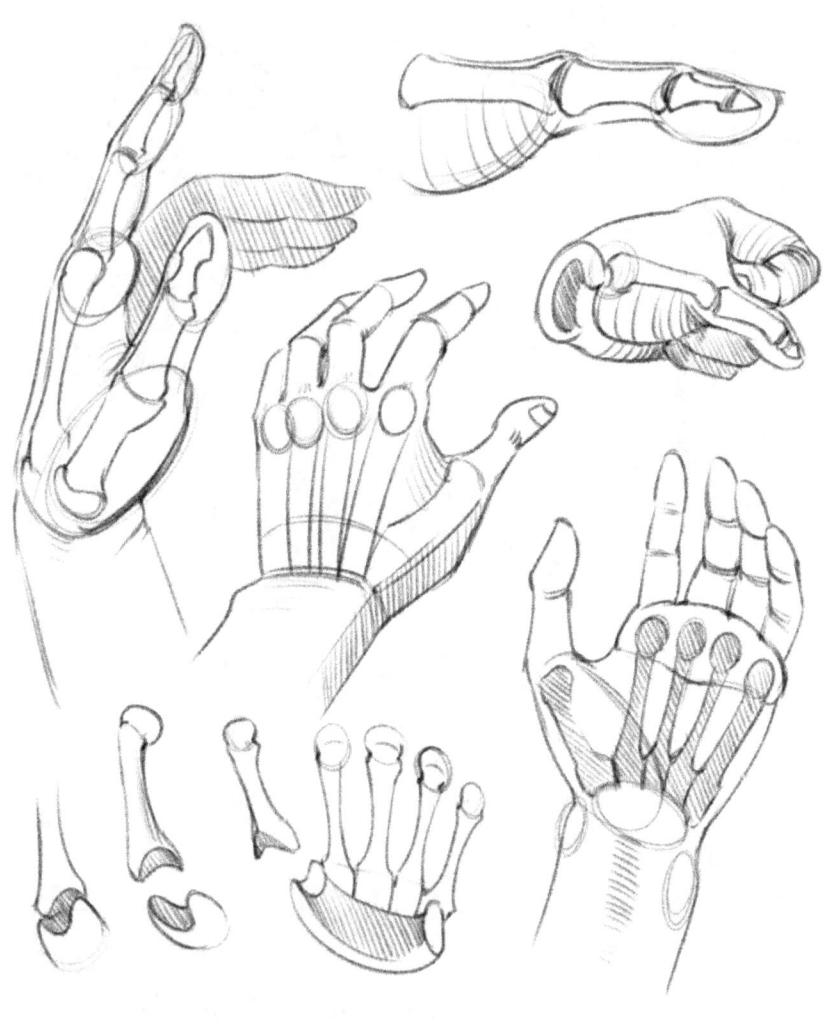

The thumb is different from the other fingers and starts on the inside of the wrist. Side of the hand It is also shown with 3 cylinders, but only has 2 phalanges. The main first cylinder is the carpal bone, which is more mobile and differs from the others, which are connected in the same plane with each other. It has a so-called saddle joint, which gives the thumb greater mobility.

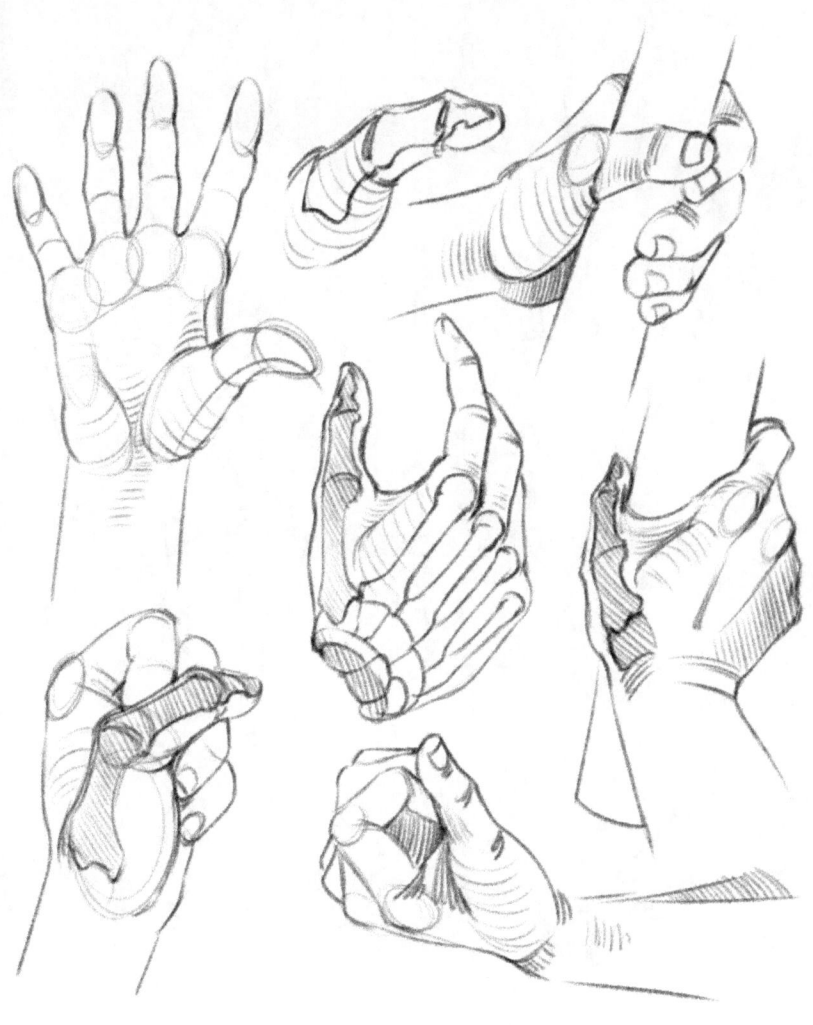

The saddle joint is located on the edge of the wrist and opposes the fingers when the fist is closed. Therefore, the thumb is opposable, that is, it can move in the opposite direction from the other fingers. It allows us to hold and squeeze objects, and grasp and move them. The other fingers of the hand are not opposable, so they cannot perform these actions as effectively.

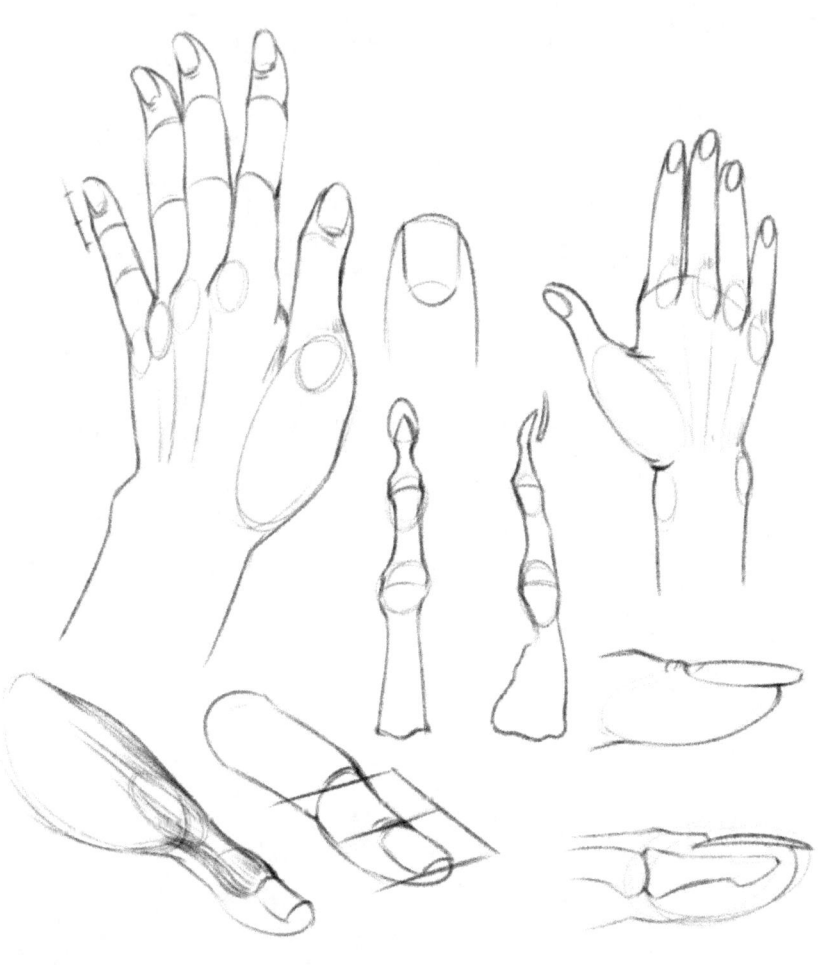

It is worth paying attention to the tips of the fingers, namely the nails - hard plates that cover the distal phalanges of the fingers and toes and protect the tips of the fingers from damage. They are hard, durable, and have a smooth surface.

The nail plate is the visible part of the nail. Occupies approximately half the length of the phalanx. Under the plate is the nail bed.

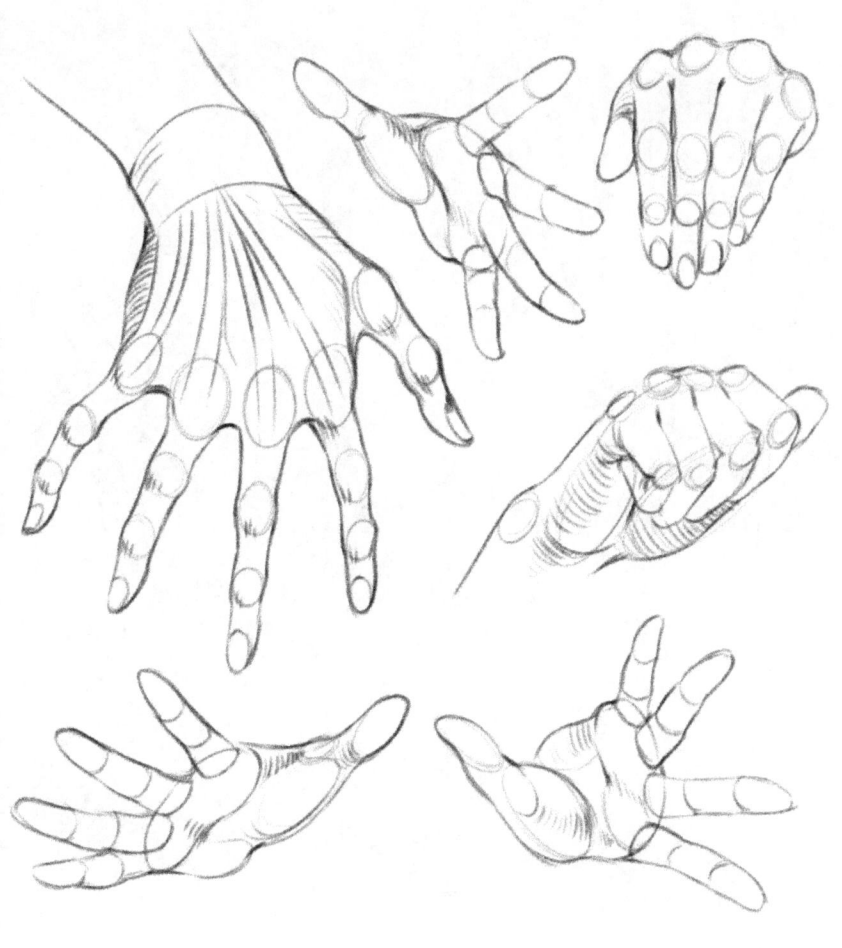

The joints of the metacarpals and phalanges form spherical points that help maintain the placement of the main elements of the hand.

First, you can draw the plane of the palm, and mark the main rounded fleshy masses on it. Then place the starting points of the phalanges, and add the phalanges of the fingers and nails. This simple scheme will help to depict the movements of fingers and hands in perspective.

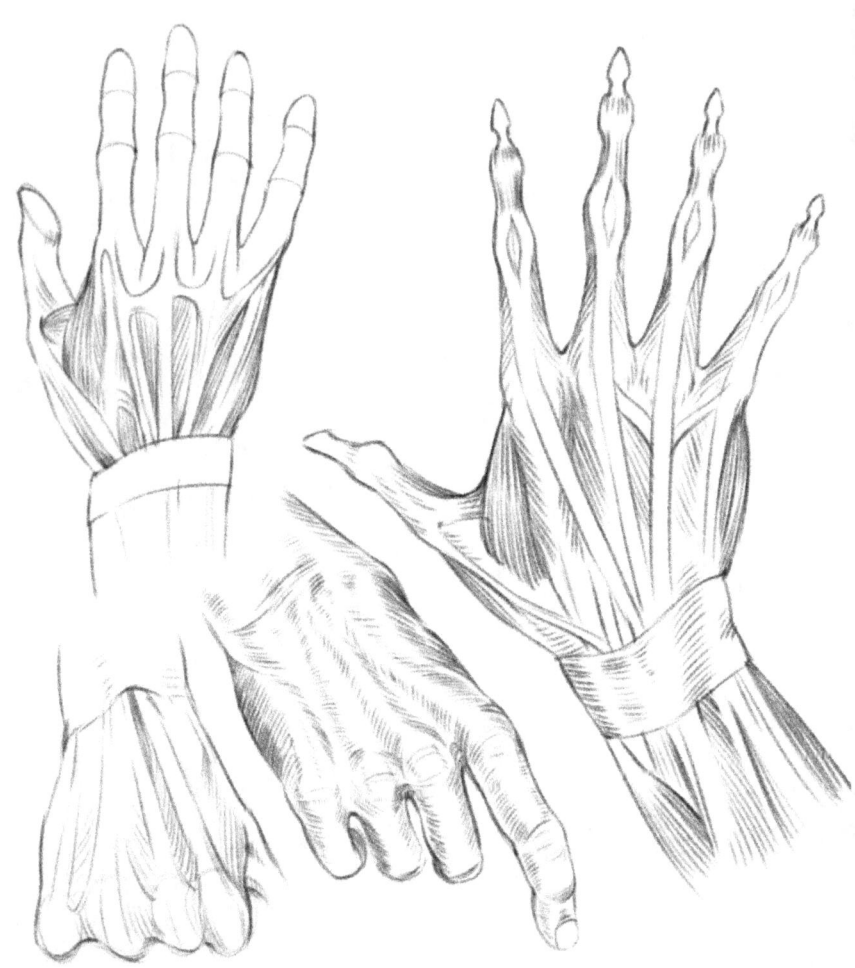

The extensors of the hands pass along the back - a group of muscles that are responsible for extending the fingers. They are located on the back surface of the forearm and are connected to the bones of the fingers with the help of tendons. These tendons form visible lines on the surface and conditionally pass along the line of the metatarsal bones.

They are especially noticeable when we spread our fingers or bend our hand into a fist. In thin or older people, the skin on the hands is thinner, which also makes the tendon lines on the back of the hand more visible.

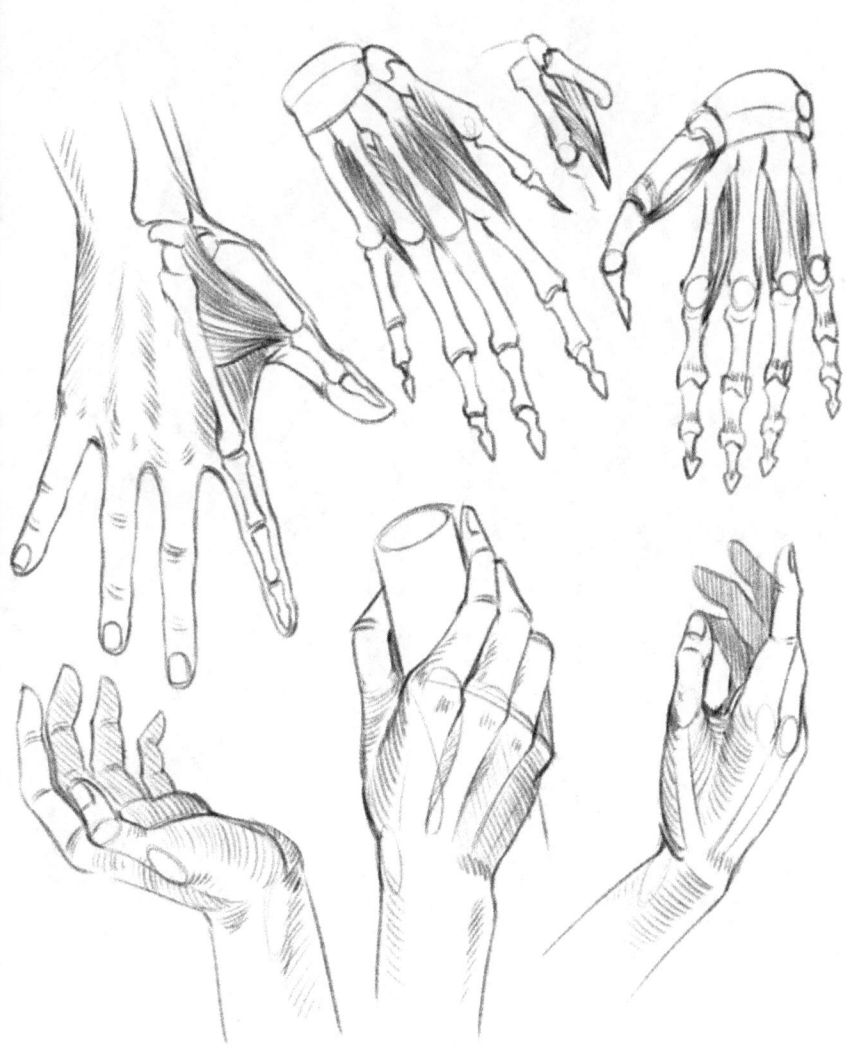

Interosseous muscles are located on the metacarpal bones of the hand. They are responsible for bending and extending the fingers in the interphalangeal joints. They are connected to the bones of the fingers with the help of tendons. The interosseous muscles of the hand ensure smooth and precise movement of the fingers. The thumb has additional muscles that are responsible for its movements and have noticeable differences in structure (they are wider and longer). These muscles are located in the thickness of the thumb and are connected to the bones of the thumb by means of tendons.

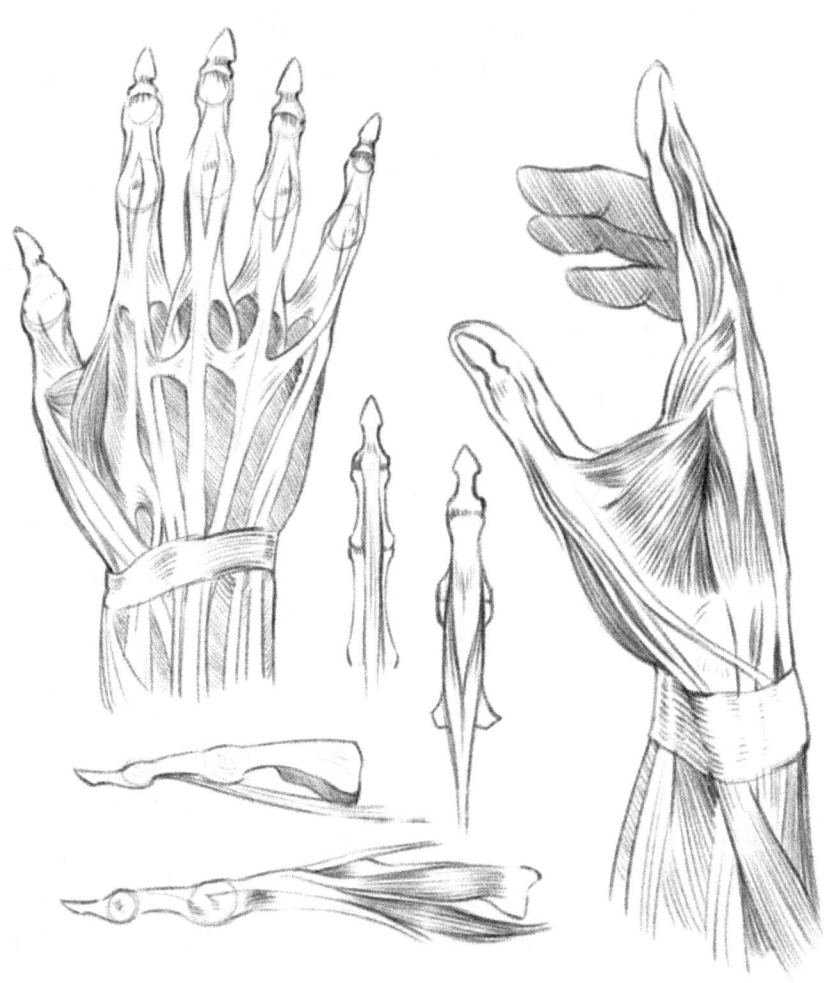

The tendons of the muscles of the hand can cover the bones of the fingers in different ways. Some tendons cover bones on only one side. Other tendons cover the bones on both sides, forming a loop. The flexors of the fingers have short tendons that attach directly to the phalanges of the fingers. The extensors of the fingers have long tendons that pass through the canals in the carpal bones and then through the canals in the metatarsal bones.

The thumb has the same muscles as the other fingers, except for the opposable thumb muscle, which is responsible for opposing the thumb to the other fingers.

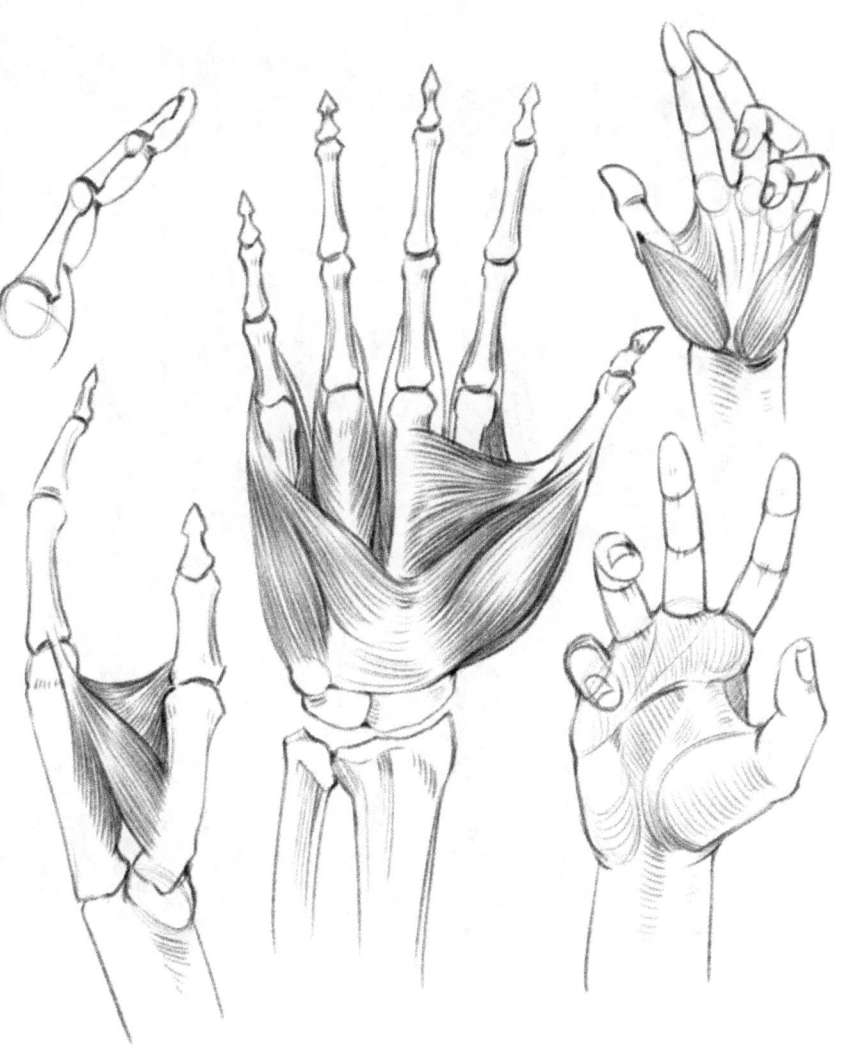

The palm is voluminous near the thumb and on the side of the little finger due to the fact that in these places there are large muscles that are responsible for the movements of these fingers.

The opposite muscles, flexors, and extensors of the thumb form a pear-shaped shape at the base of the thumb. The abductor muscle connects the thumb with the second and third metatarsal bones. On the side of the little finger, there are also flexors and extensors, which are large and powerful, so they create volume in this part of the palm.

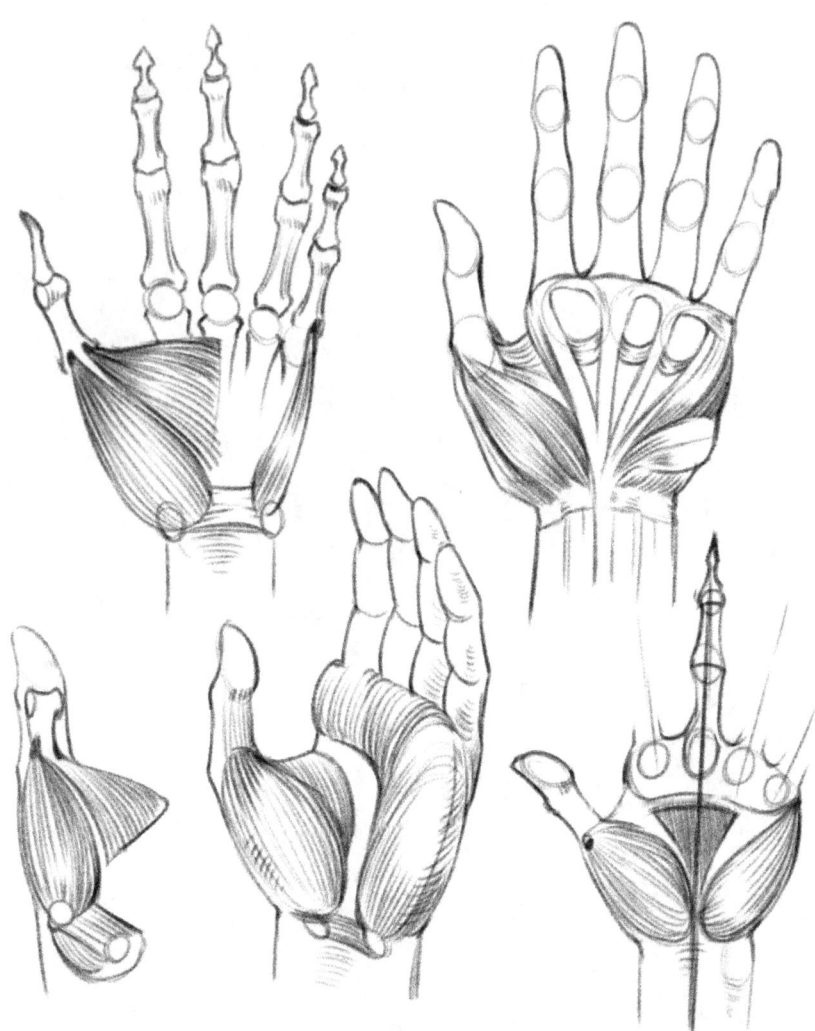

The triangular fossa in the middle of the palm is formed due to the fact that the tendons of the muscles responsible for bending the fingers pass through this area. These tendons form a loop that surrounds the bones of the metacarpal-phalangeal joints. This loop has a triangular shape and is concave in the middle of the palm.

The triangular fossa is an important anatomical formation and is used to determine the position of the carpo-phalangeal joints.

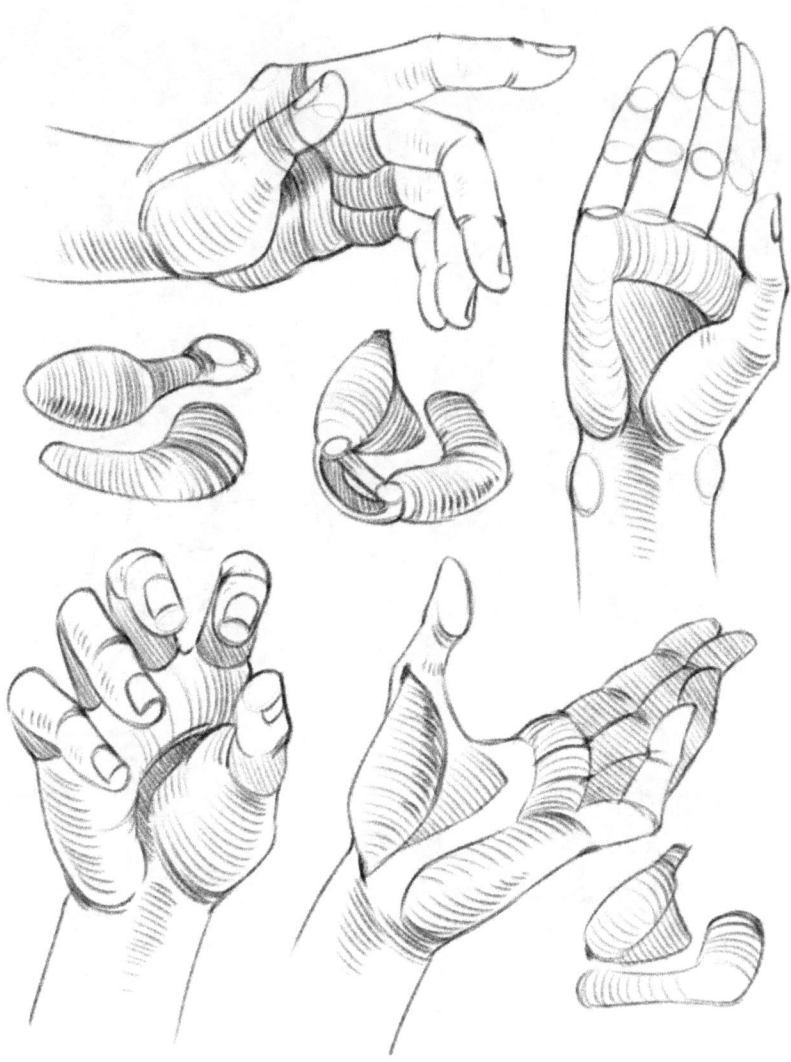

Muscle groups form two elevations on the palm surface of the hand - thenar (elevation of the thumb) and hypothenar (elevation of the little finger). They form the volume of the palm and help determine the position of the fingers. Thenar forms a projection on the palmar surface of the thumb. The hypothenar forms a less pronounced protrusion on the palmar surface of the little finger. This protrusion is clearly visible when the little finger is fully extended. The pads at the base of the fingers also contribute to the formation of the volume of the palm.

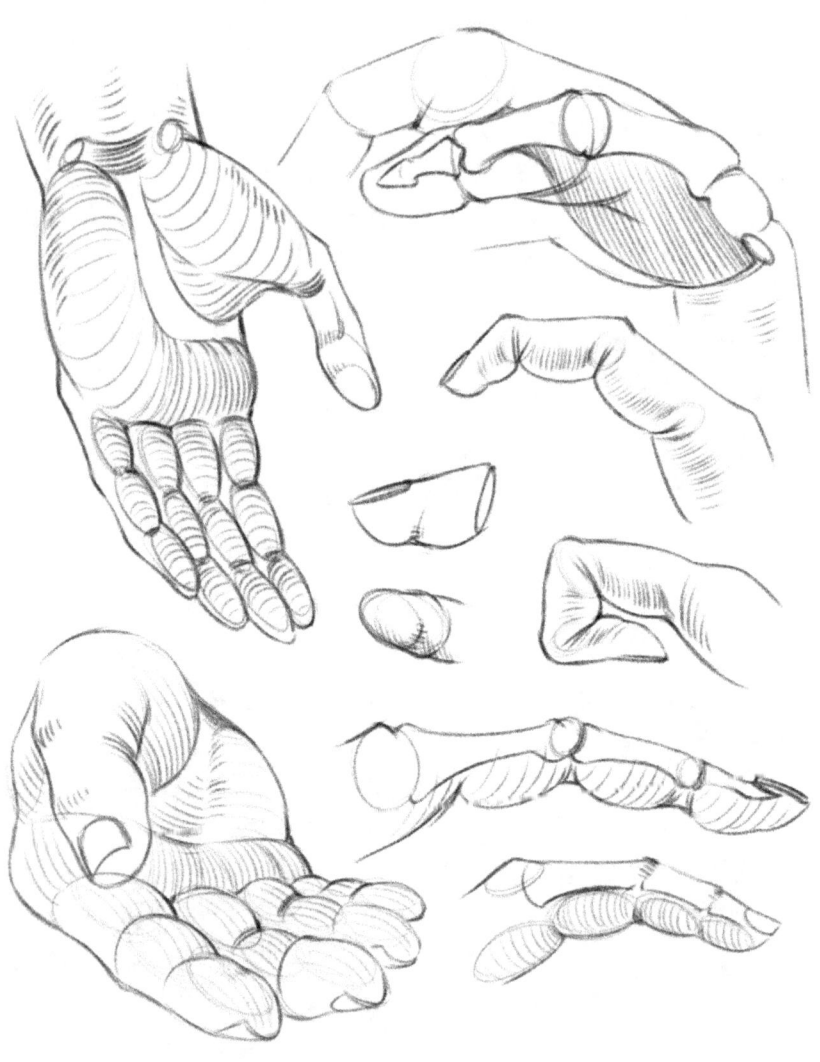

The inner part of the brush has a soft base, which is represented by rounded shapes. These forms form many dimples and folds that are more visible when the arm is bent and less when the arm is straightened. Fat people or children also have more noticeable folds.

Pay attention to how the skin bends between the phalanges of the fingers. The nail phalanx also has an inconspicuous fold formed by the sensitive pad of the fingertip.

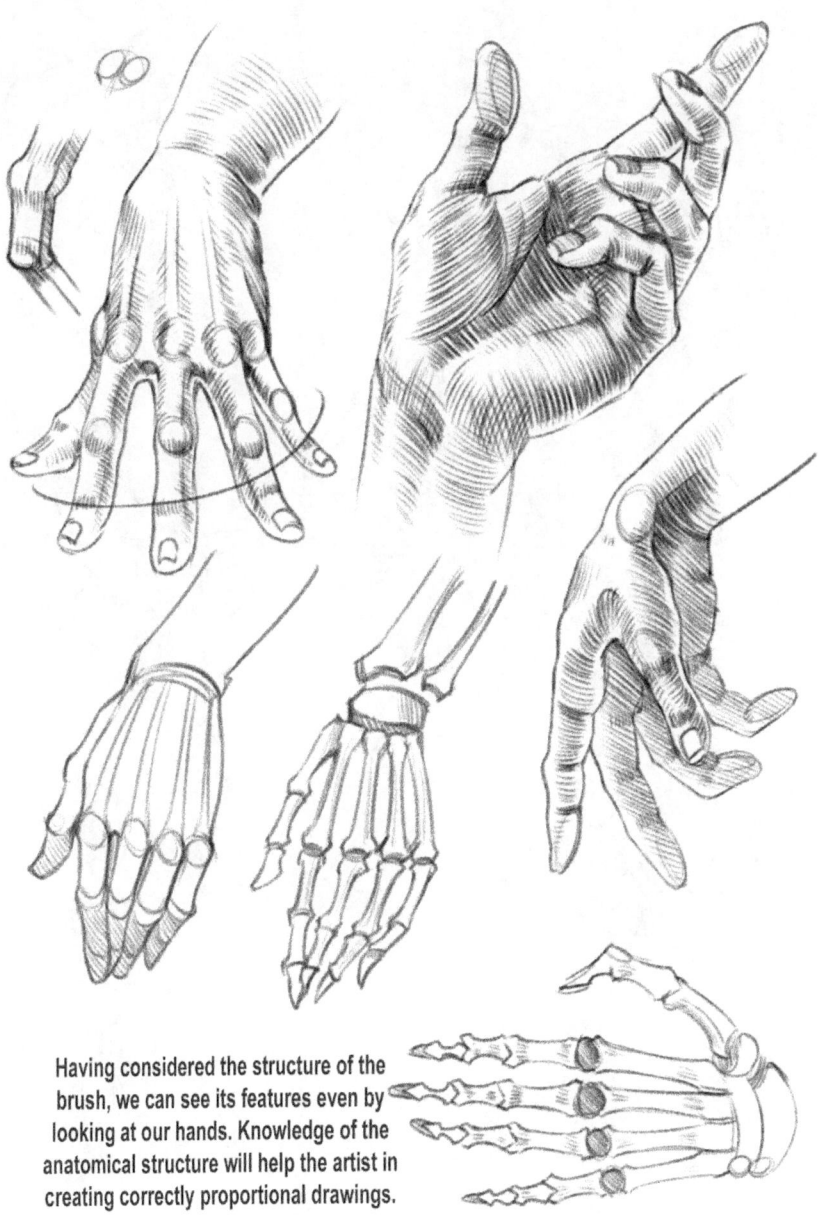

Having considered the structure of the brush, we can see its features even by looking at our hands. Knowledge of the anatomical structure will help the artist in creating correctly proportional drawings.

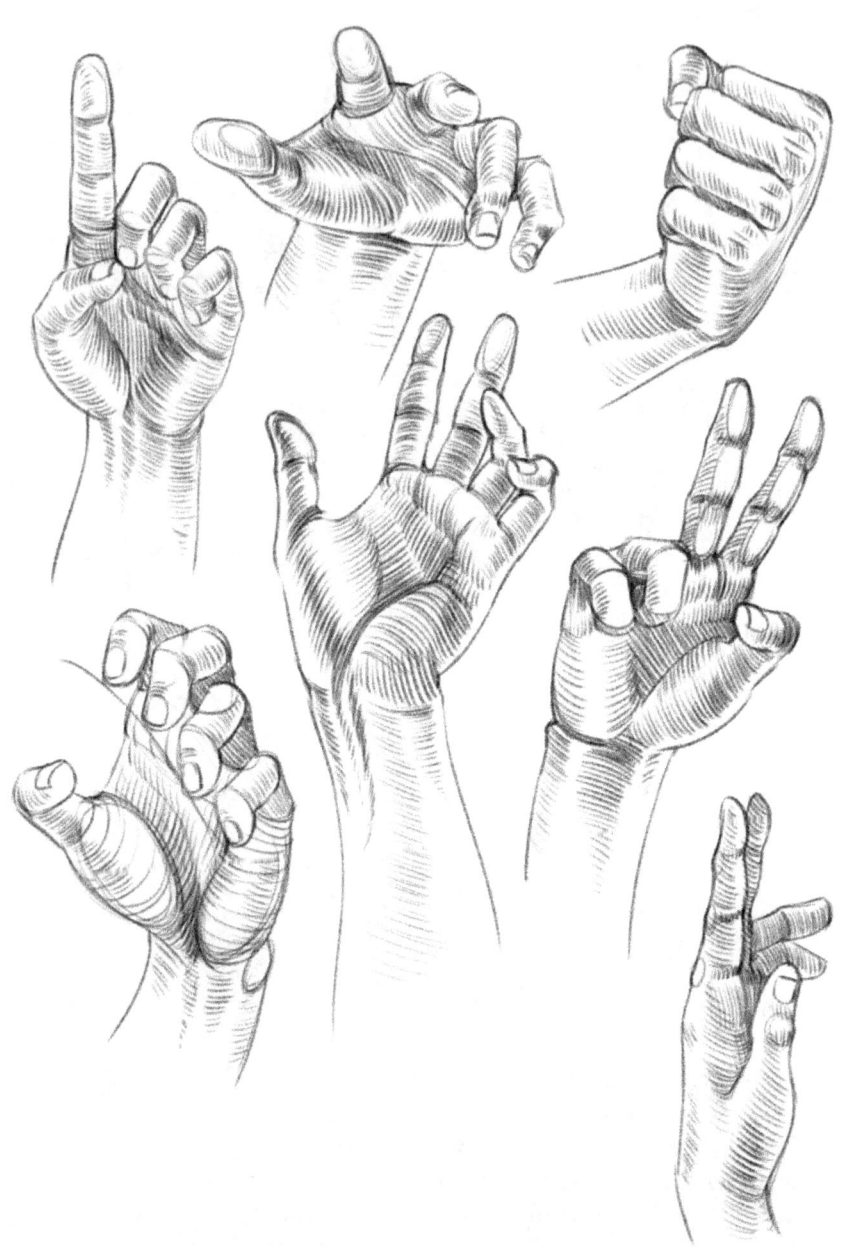

Practice is very important for an artist. By looking at the image of the hands and noticing the key features of the structure, you will be able to learn how to draw such a complex part of the body.

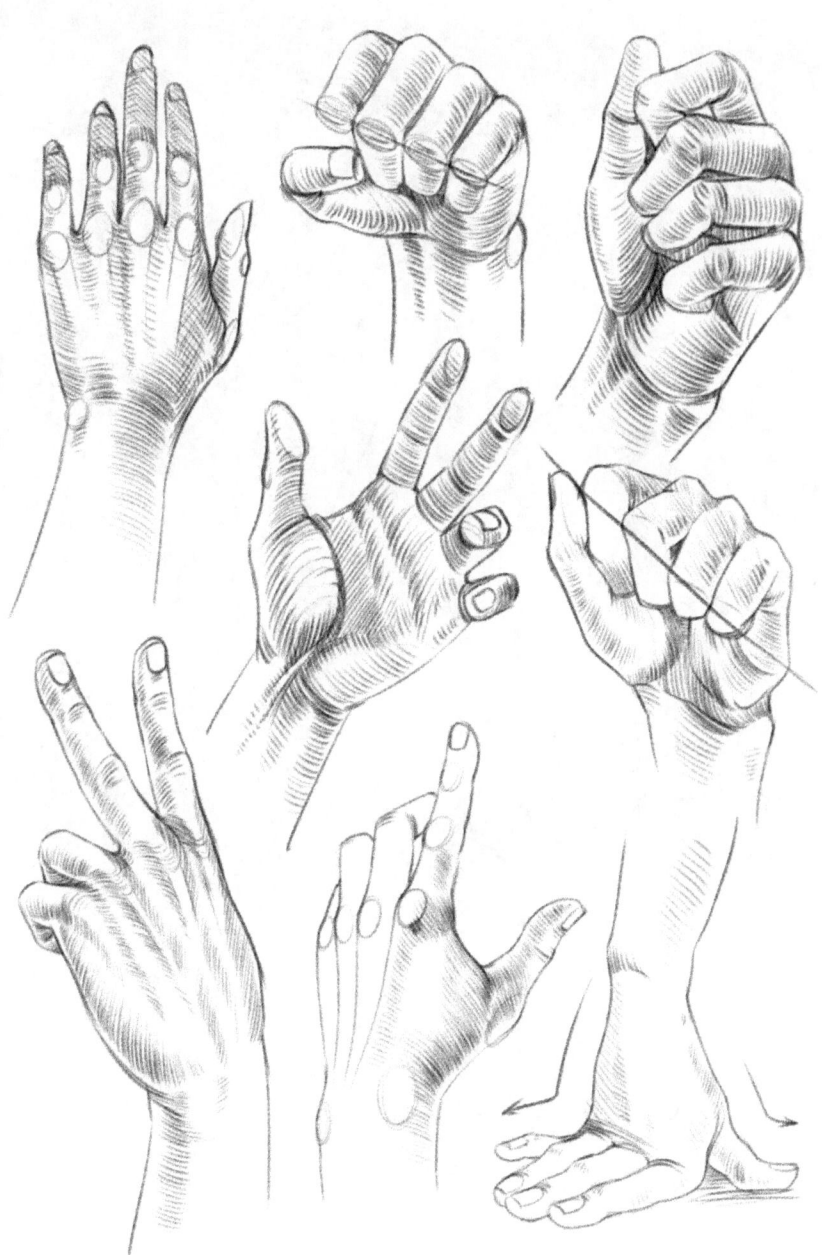

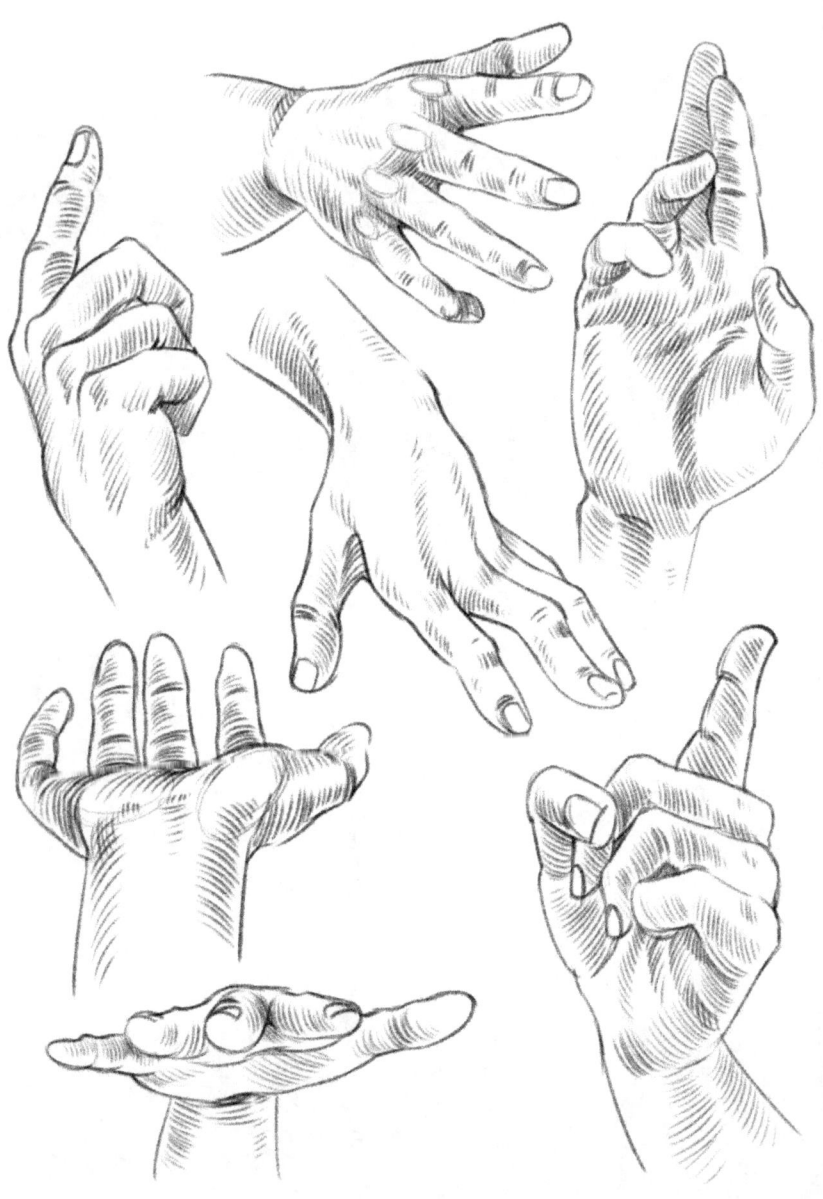

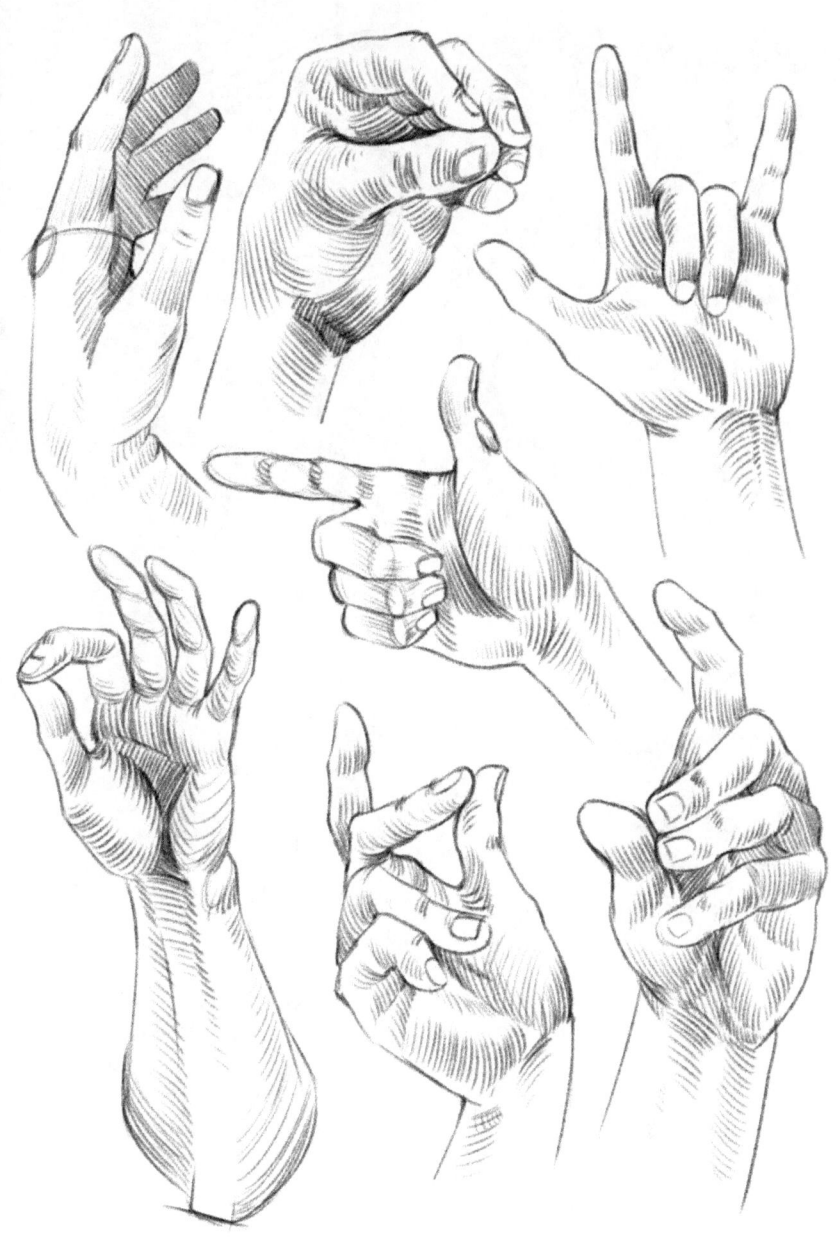

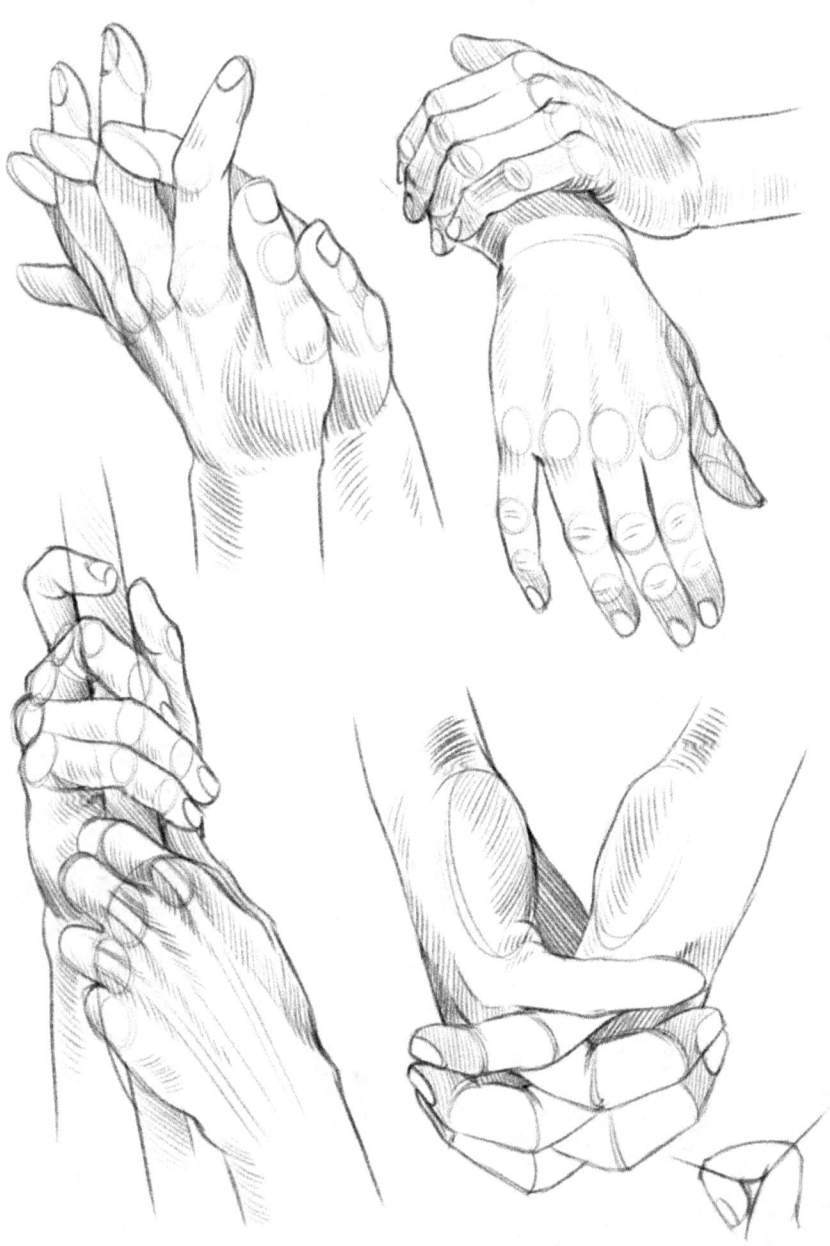

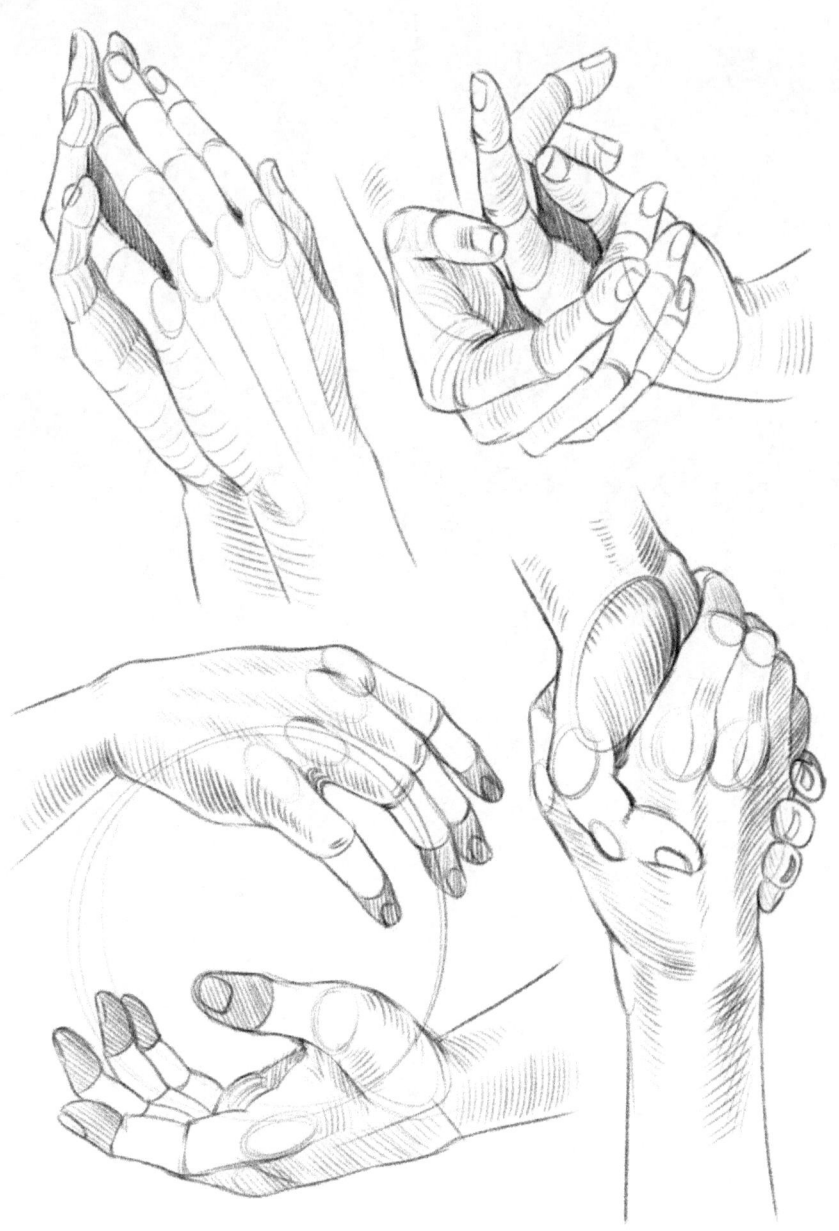

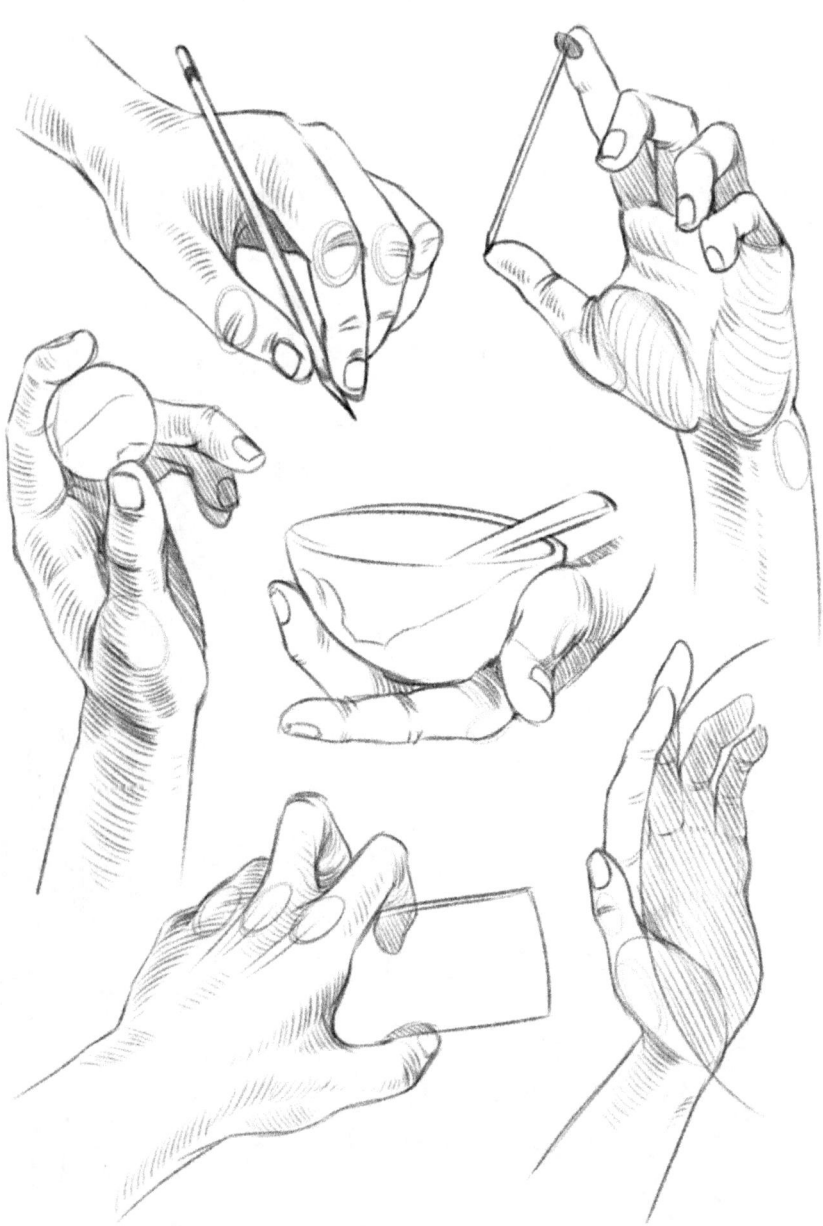

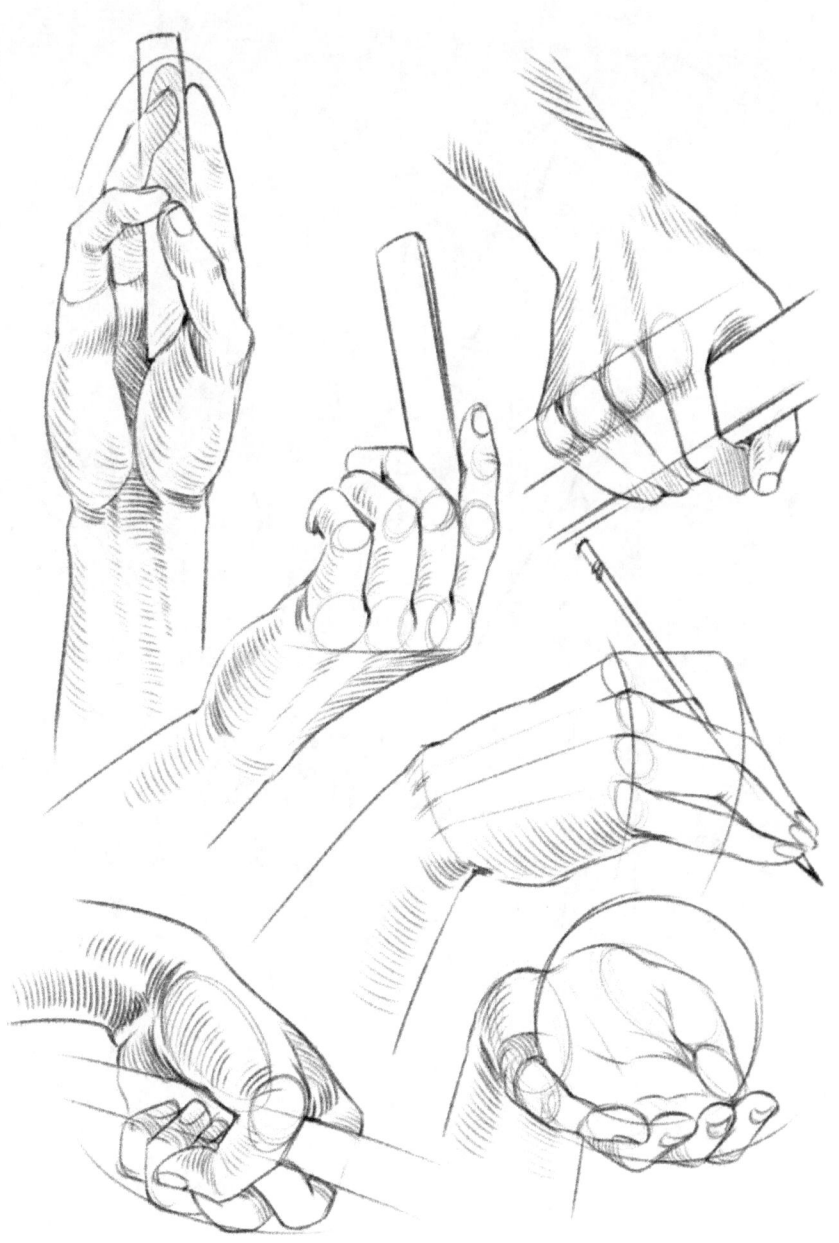

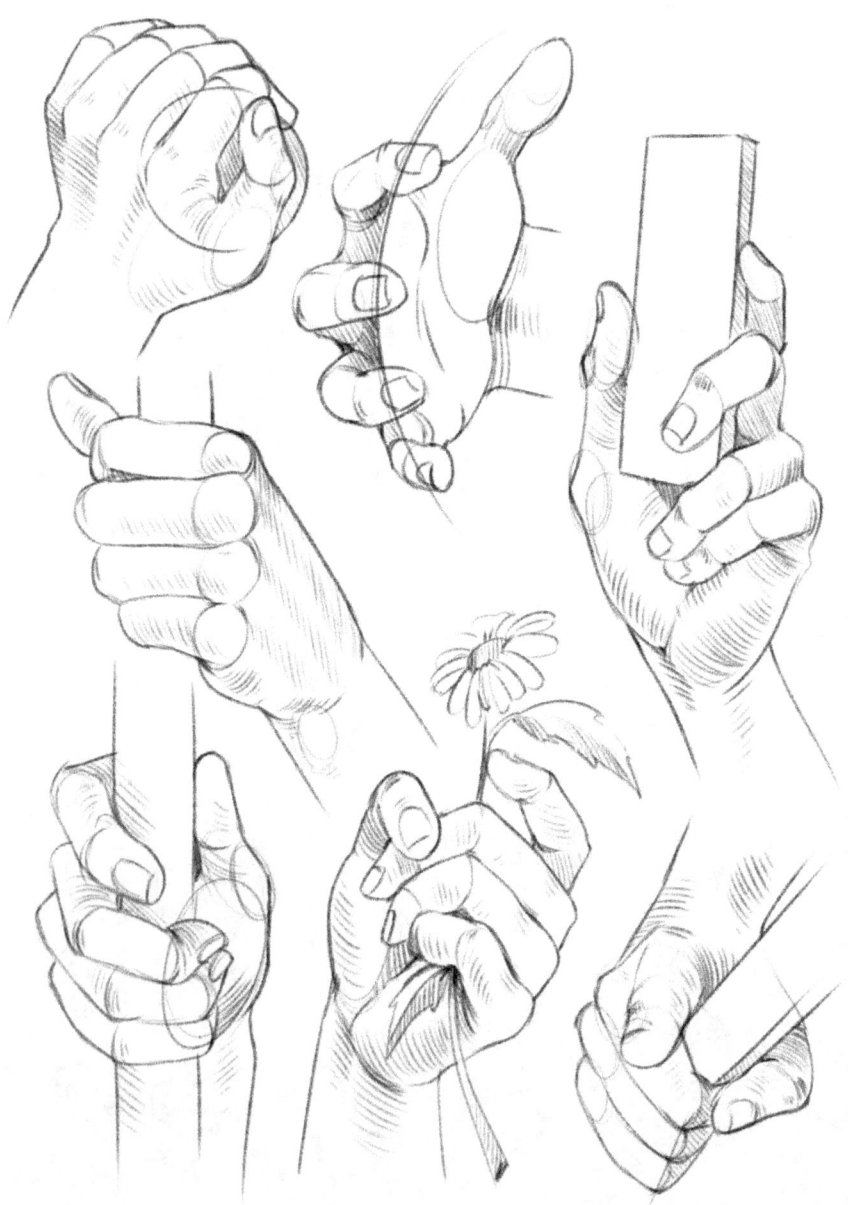

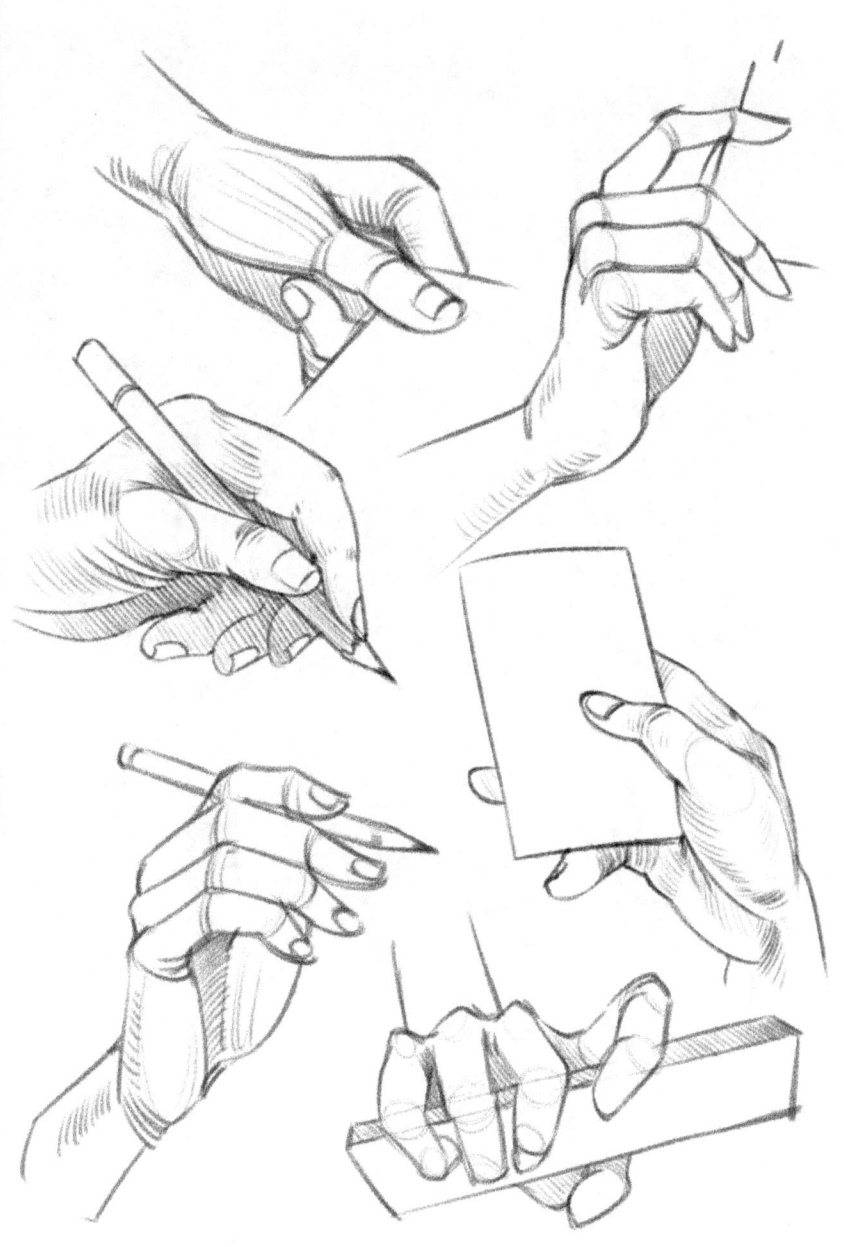

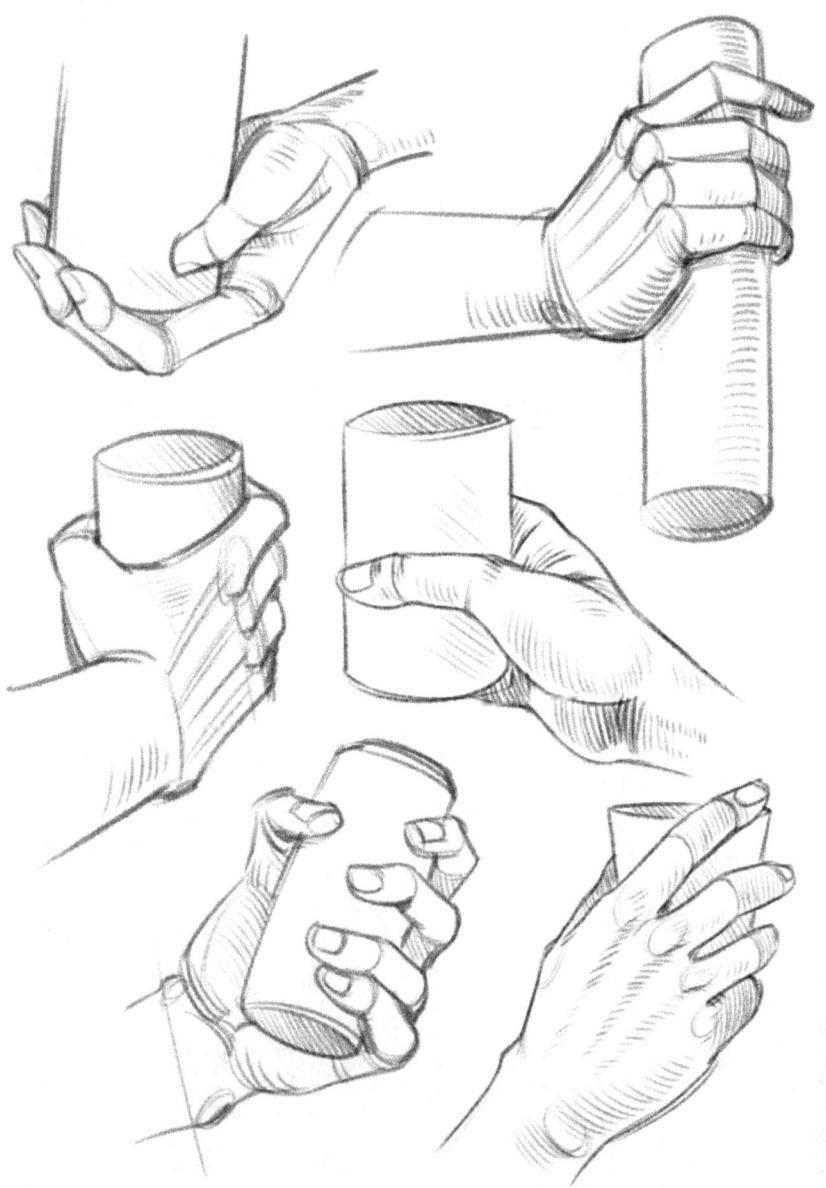

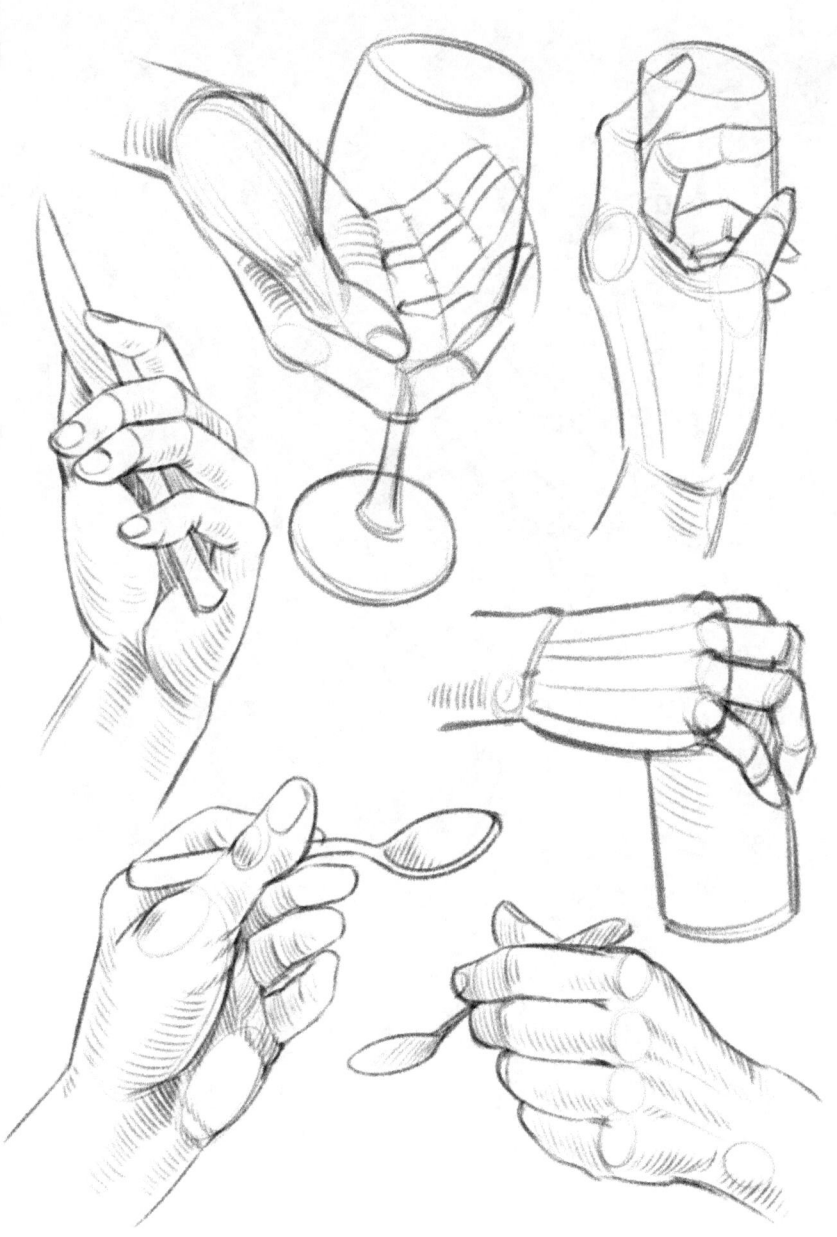

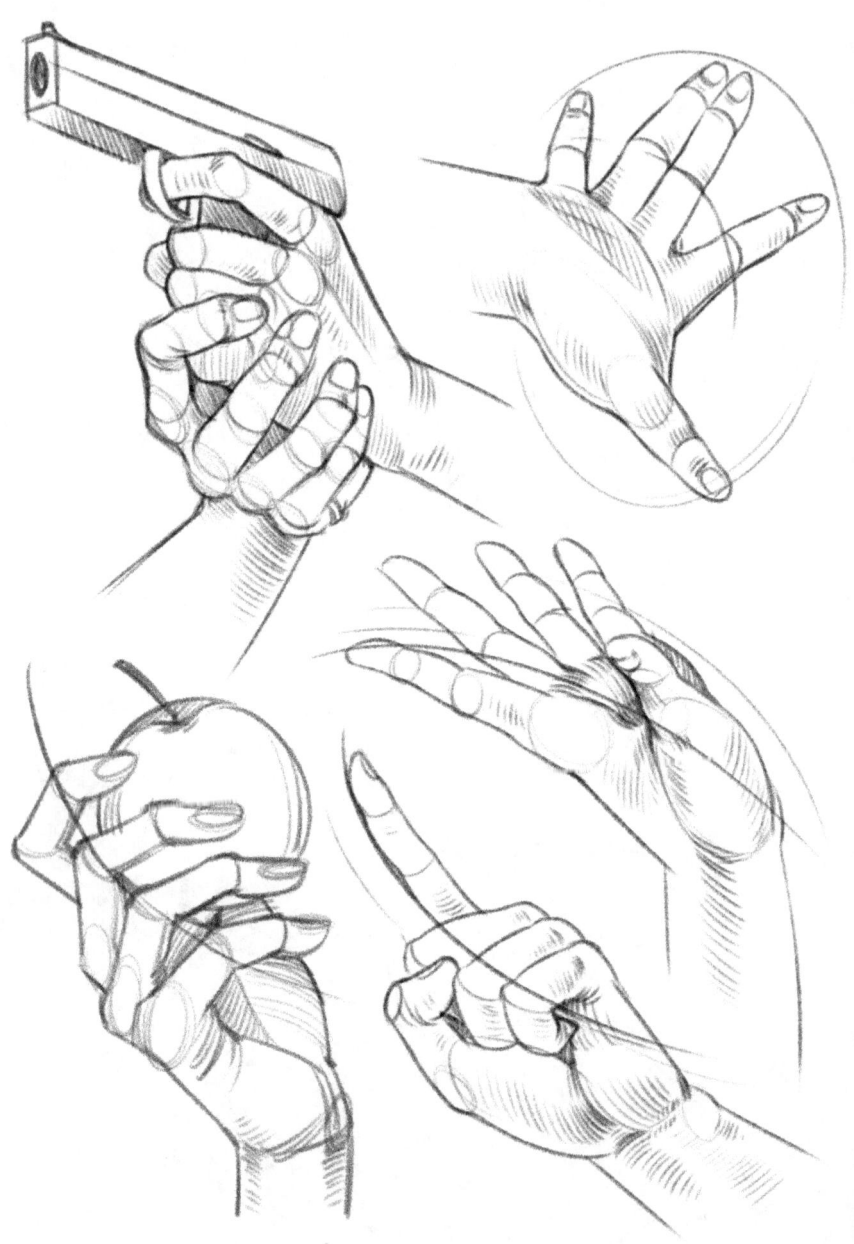

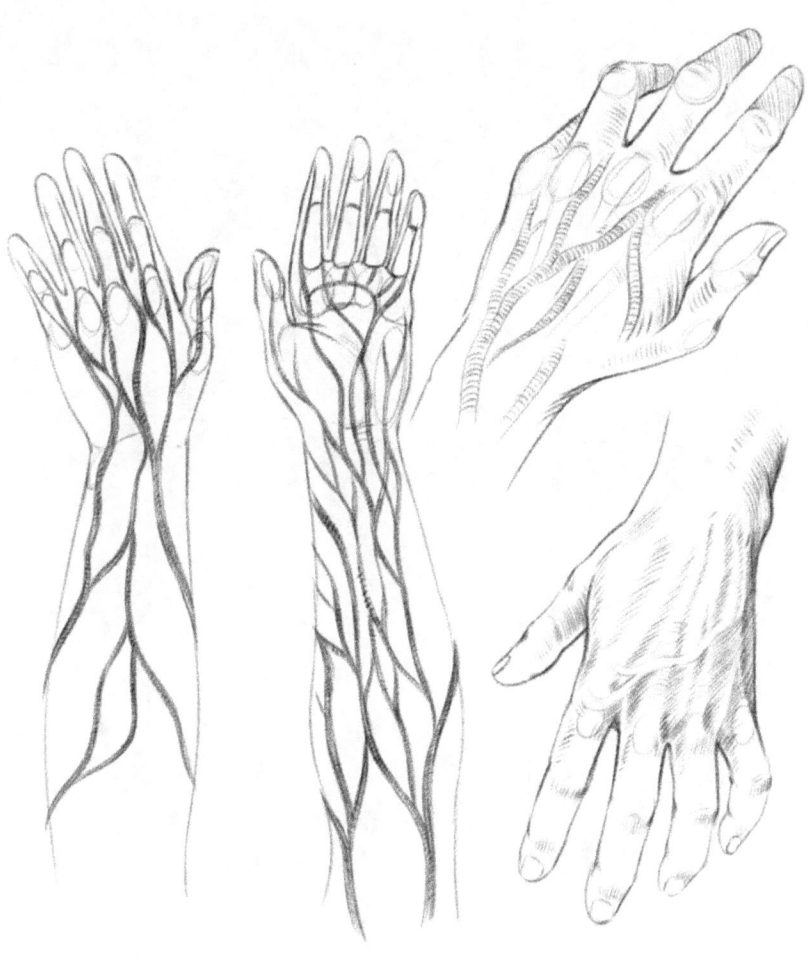

The hands of old people have a number of characteristic features that distinguish them from the hands of young people. With age, the muscle mass in the hands and the amount of subcutaneous fat decreases. The skin of old people becomes thin and flabby, it loses its elasticity. This leads to the veins on the hands becoming more visible.

Protruding veins can be of different sizes and shapes. They can be thin and long, thick and short, straight or winding. They can also be noticeable in thin or fit people.

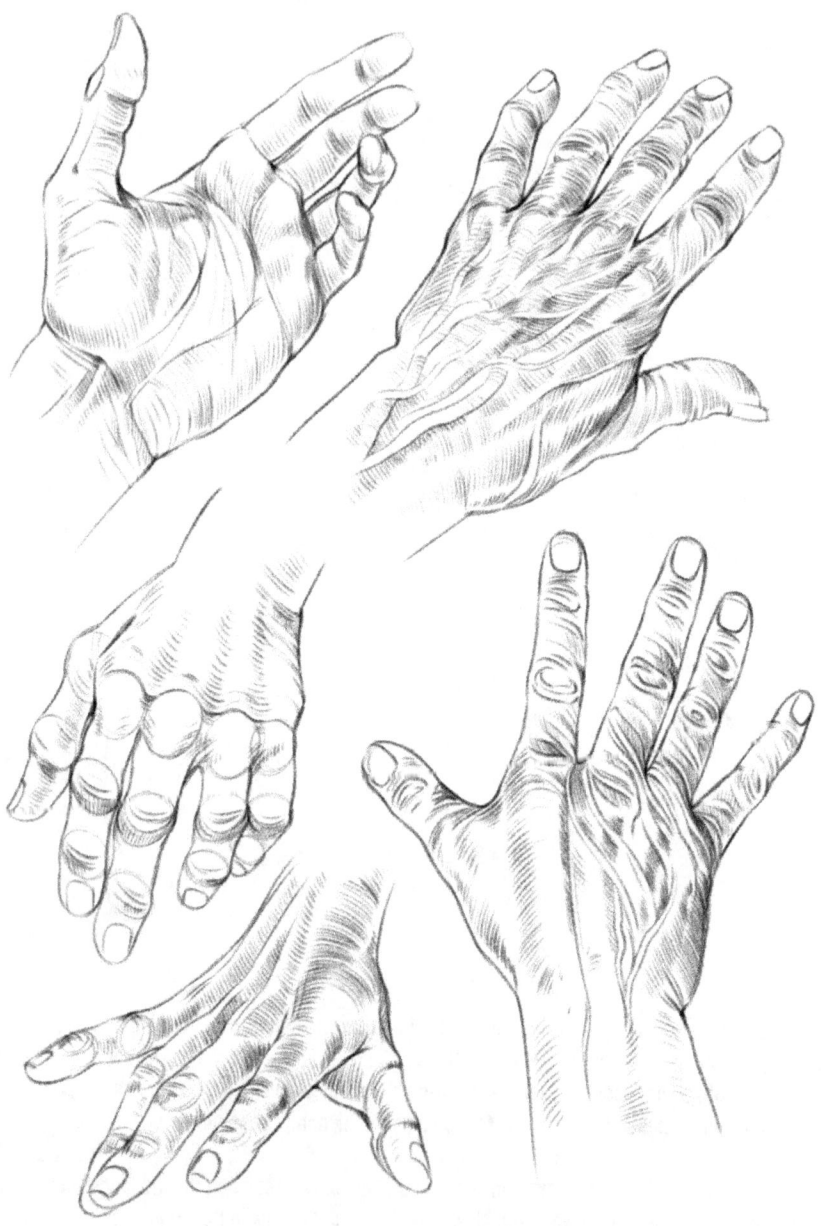

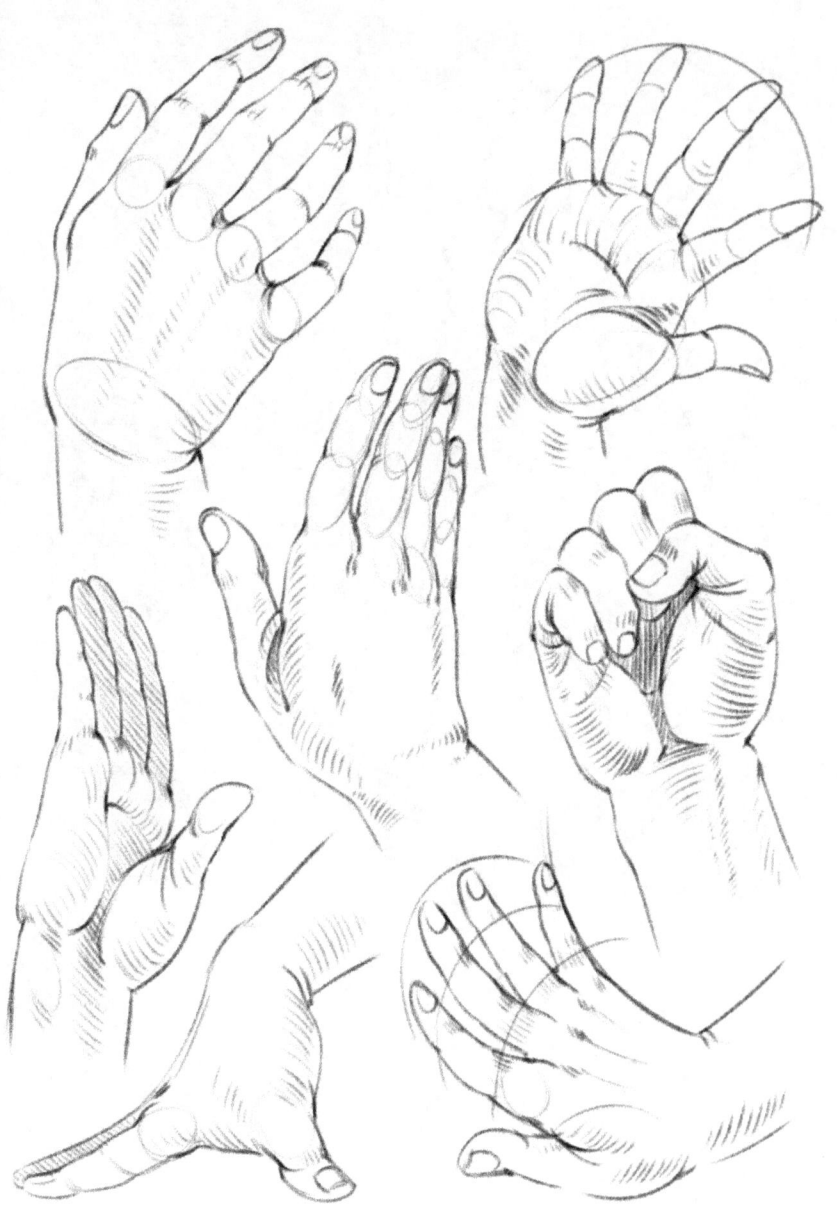

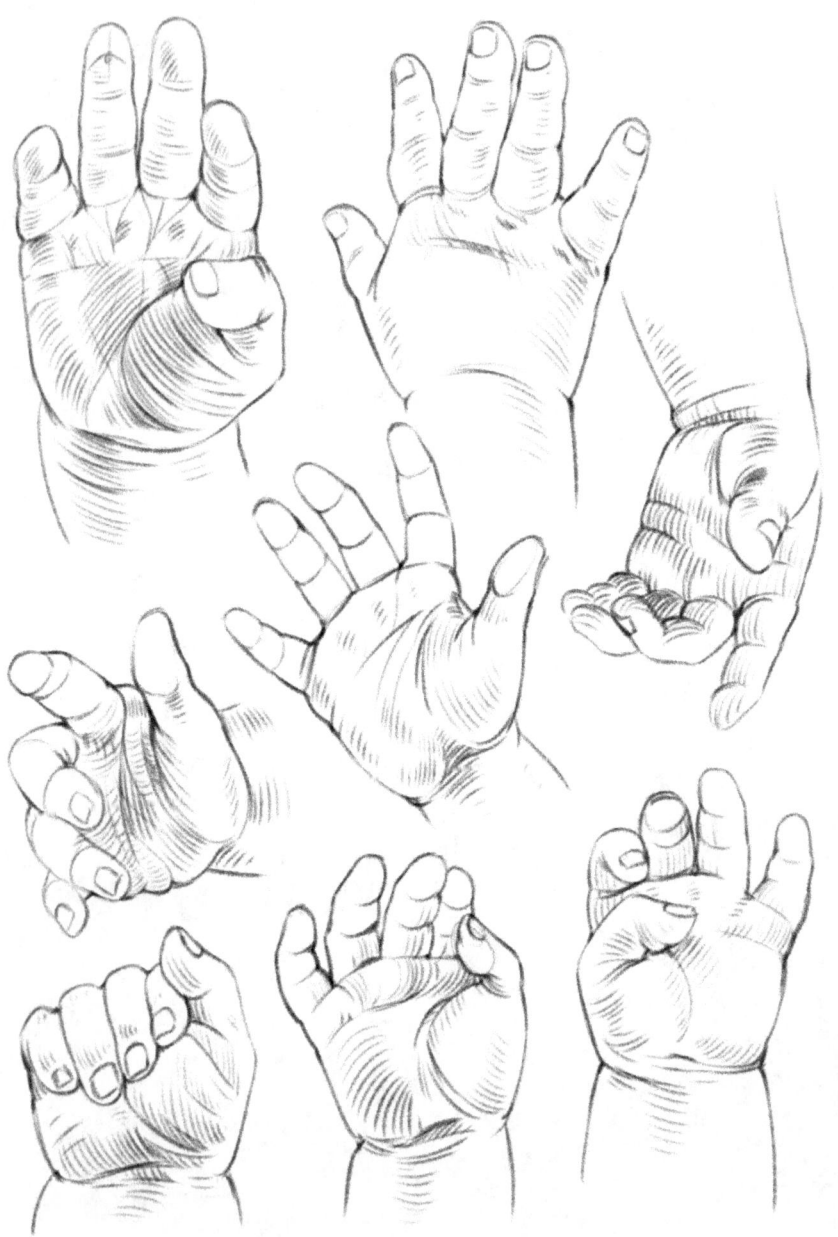

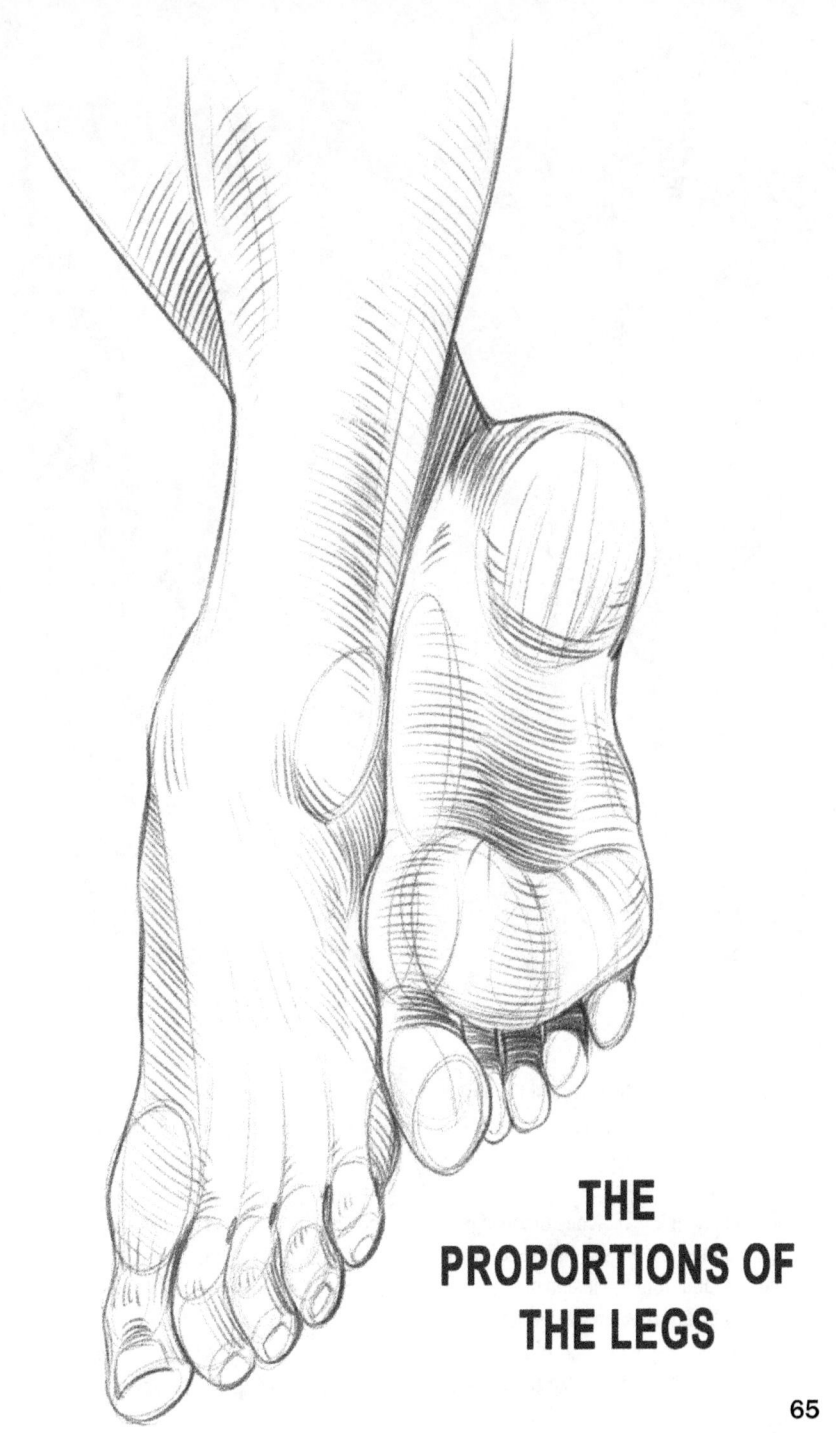

THE PROPORTIONS OF THE LEGS

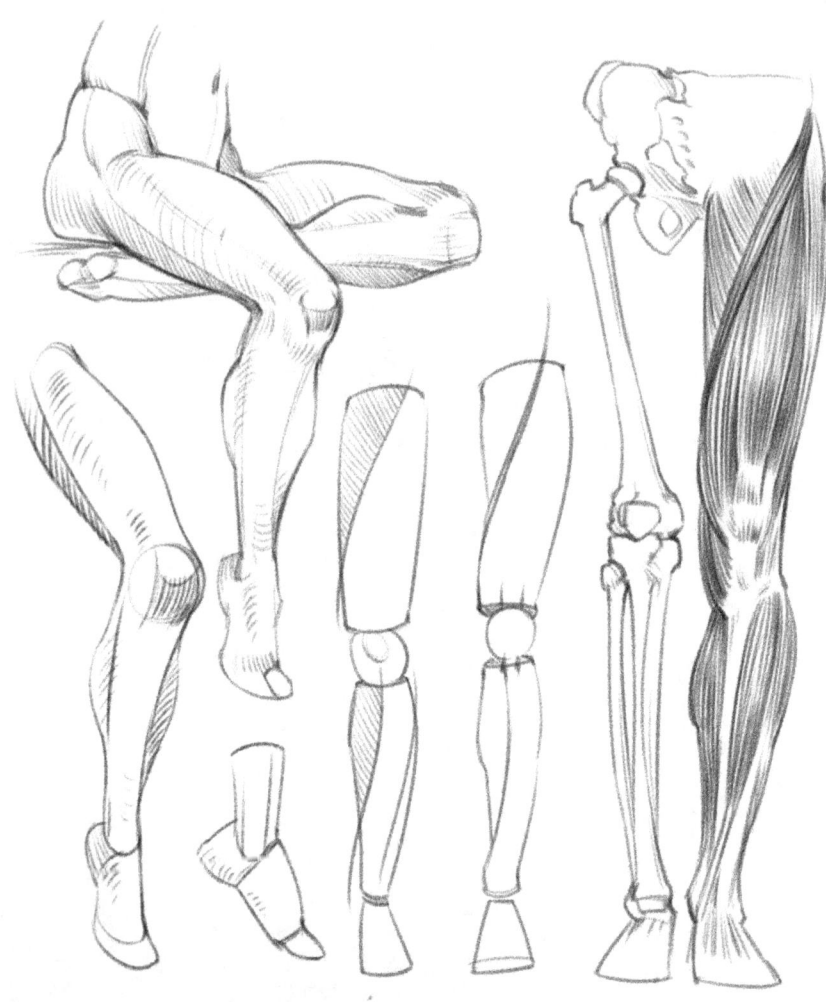

We can simplify the shape of the legs to 2 cylinders, which have a narrowing towards the bottom according to the shape of the muscles. Between them, we will place a sphere (hinge) - a knee.

If you look at the sketches of the legs, you can see the lines of muscle distribution. So from the side, we see the line of distribution of the quadriceps and biceps femoris muscle, and from the inside of the thigh - a diagonal line corresponding to the passage of the sartorius muscle, which descends from the upper corner of the pelvis and connects to the inner part of the knee. In the front part of the leg, we see a curved line from the lower leg to the ankle, which repeats the shape of the tibia.

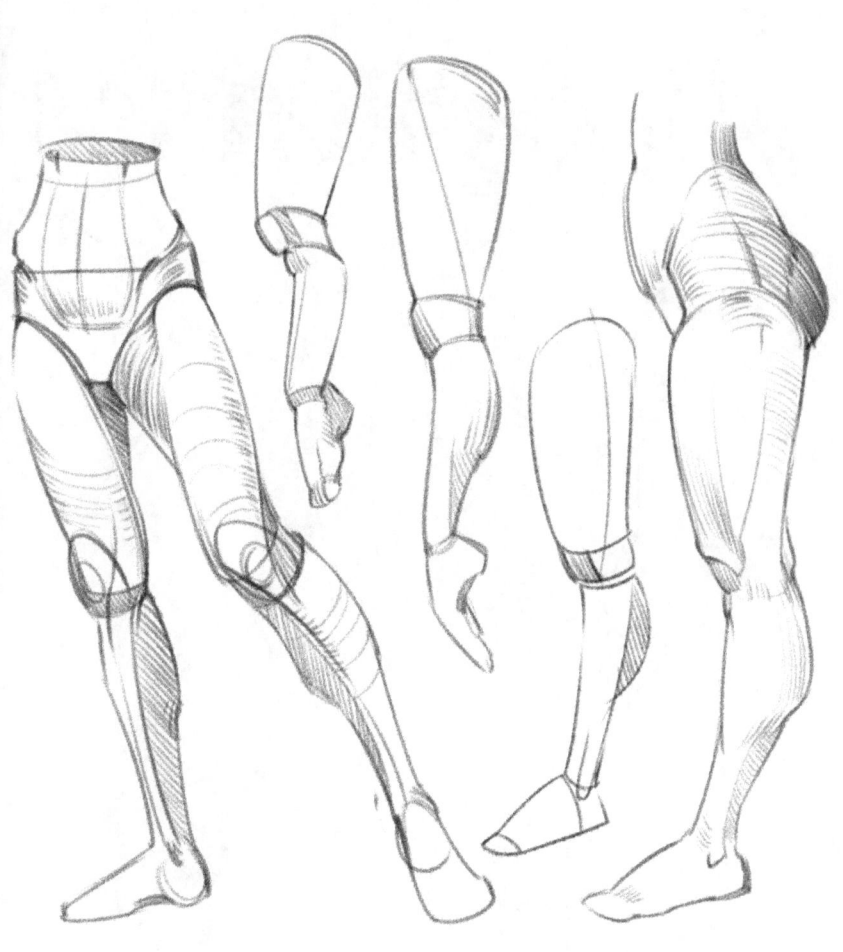

The thigh and lower leg segments are not perfectly aligned with each other. This is especially noticeable when a person stands sideways. This bending of the leg is the result of the interaction of several factors - the structure of the bones, functional features, and uneven distribution of muscle mass (the thigh has more muscle mass than the lower leg). The thigh is completely covered by muscles, especially the powerful quadriceps in the front. The calf muscle, located on the back surface of the leg, has a fairly voluminous rounded shape, while the muscles are less visible on the front surface of the leg. This contributes to the fact that the thigh goes forward and the lower leg goes back. At the same time, the knee seems to bend back.

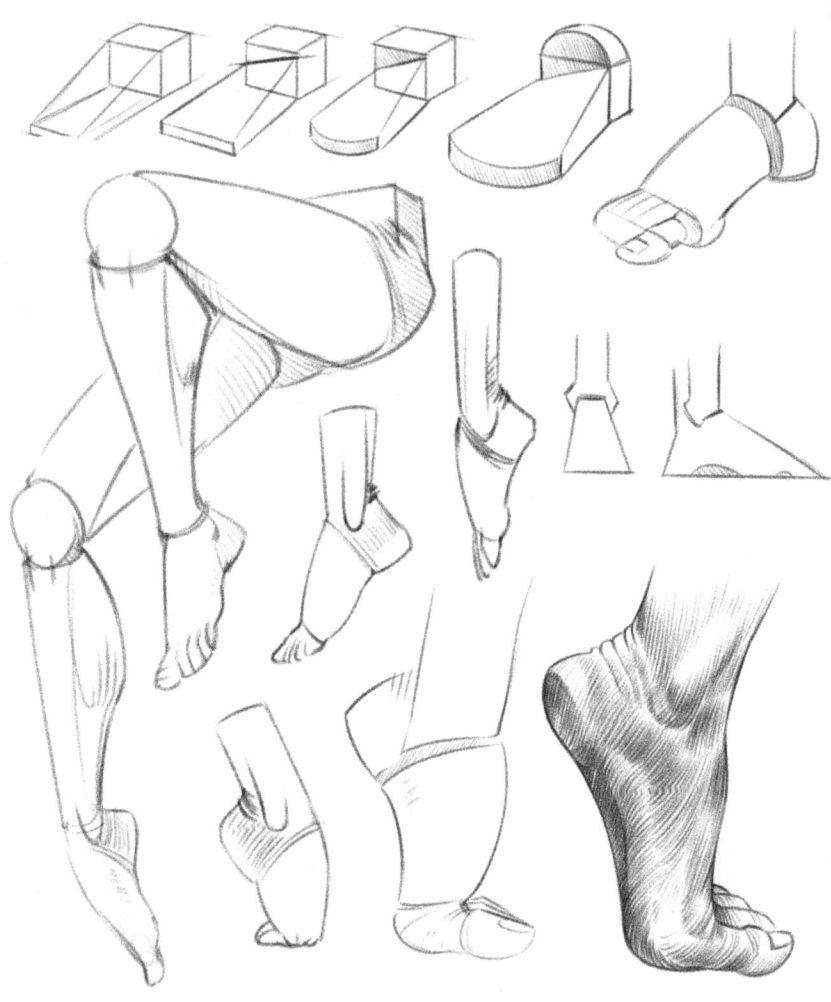

The foot is a rather complex part of the body, but it can also be simplified. Usually, we depict it as a wedge/triangle, but with greater detail - in 3 parts.

The back of the foot, the heel, has a rectangular base with a rounding at the back. The middle part of the foot is like an inclined rectangle, which has an inclination towards the outer side of the foot and the phalanx of the toes, which corresponds to the bony structure of the foot. Next, the middle part (fingers) begins, which can be divided along the line of the fingers. It can also be clarified by showing the cylinders of the phalanges and marking the volume joint of the thumb with a sofa.

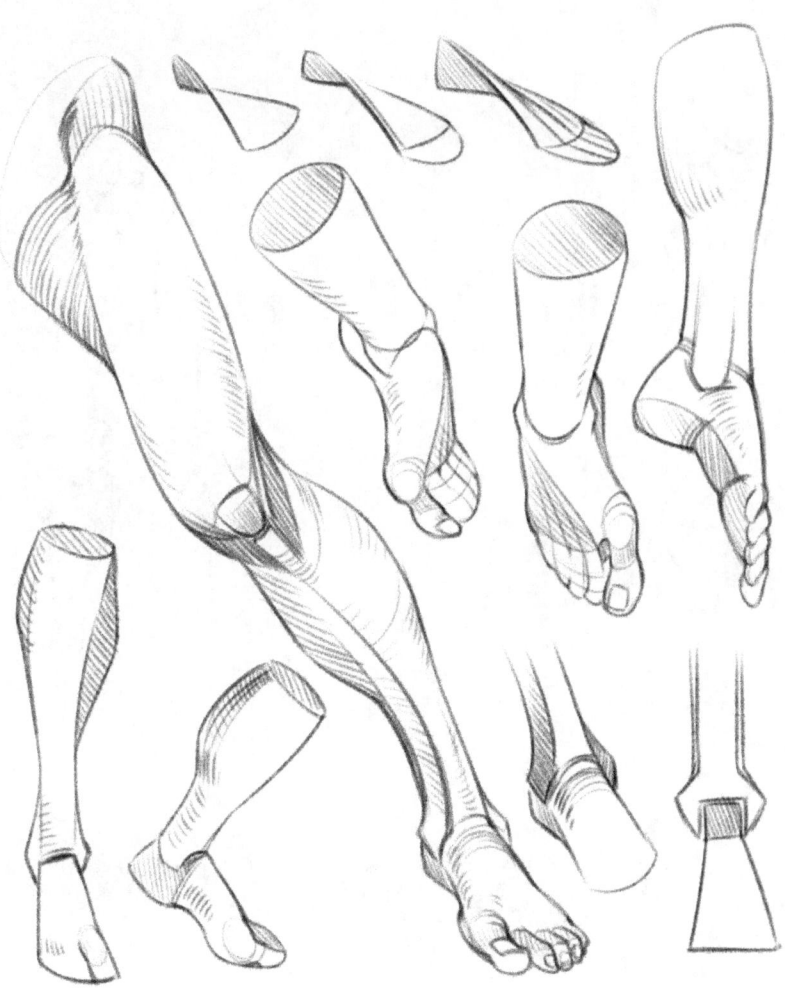

The rise of the foot can be represented by a bent plane. This is well illustrated by the arched curve of the foot, which has space in the inner part and is lowered to the outer part of the foot and the phalanges of the toes. The arch of the foot is more visible when the leg is extended or resting on the toes.

In the case of the ankle, the ligaments and muscles are arranged in such a way that they create a rounded shape. You can depict the ankle in a shape similar to a wrench. The outer articular surfaces are flat, and inside it has a niche for the talus. This allows it to move in different directions while providing stability to the ankle.

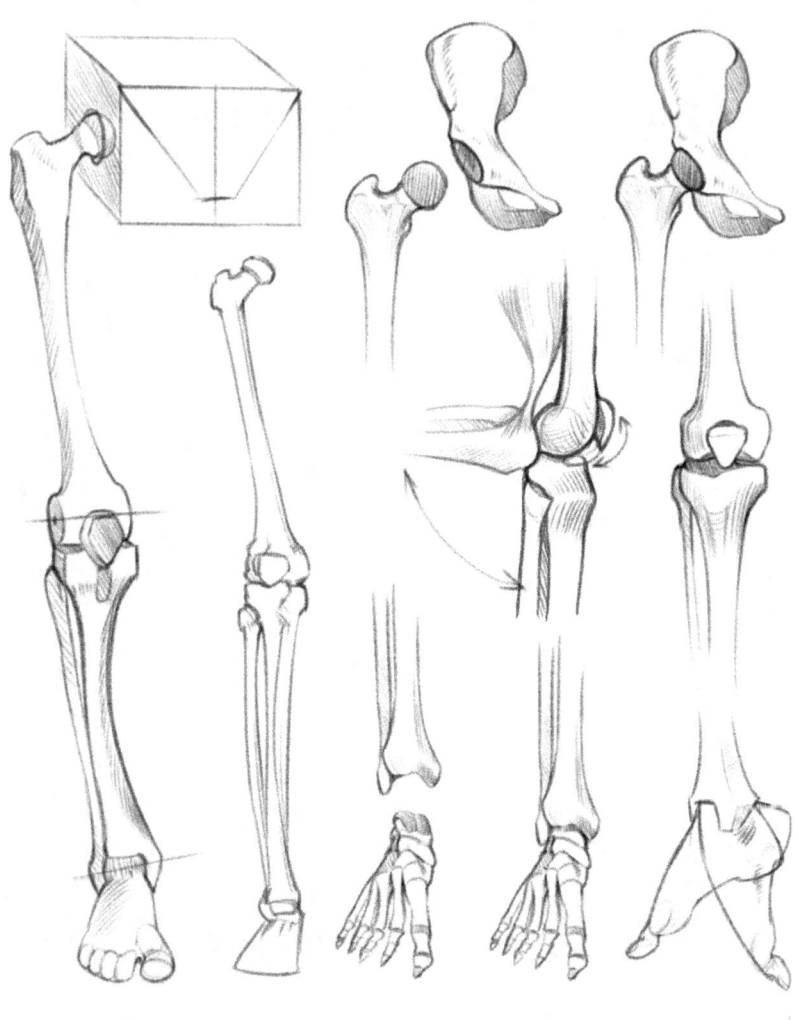

Joints consist of bones connected by ligaments and muscles. Ligaments and muscles help to stabilize the joint and ensure its mobility.

The femoral (hip) joint has the form of a hinge that moves in a curved plane, rotating in different directions. The knee joint is a complex joint that connects the main bones of the leg and ensures the bending and extension of the leg (back and forth). The ankle-foot joint is like a wrench and provides flexion and extension of the foot, external and internal rotation of the foot, and inclination of the foot up and down, while firmly fixing the foot.

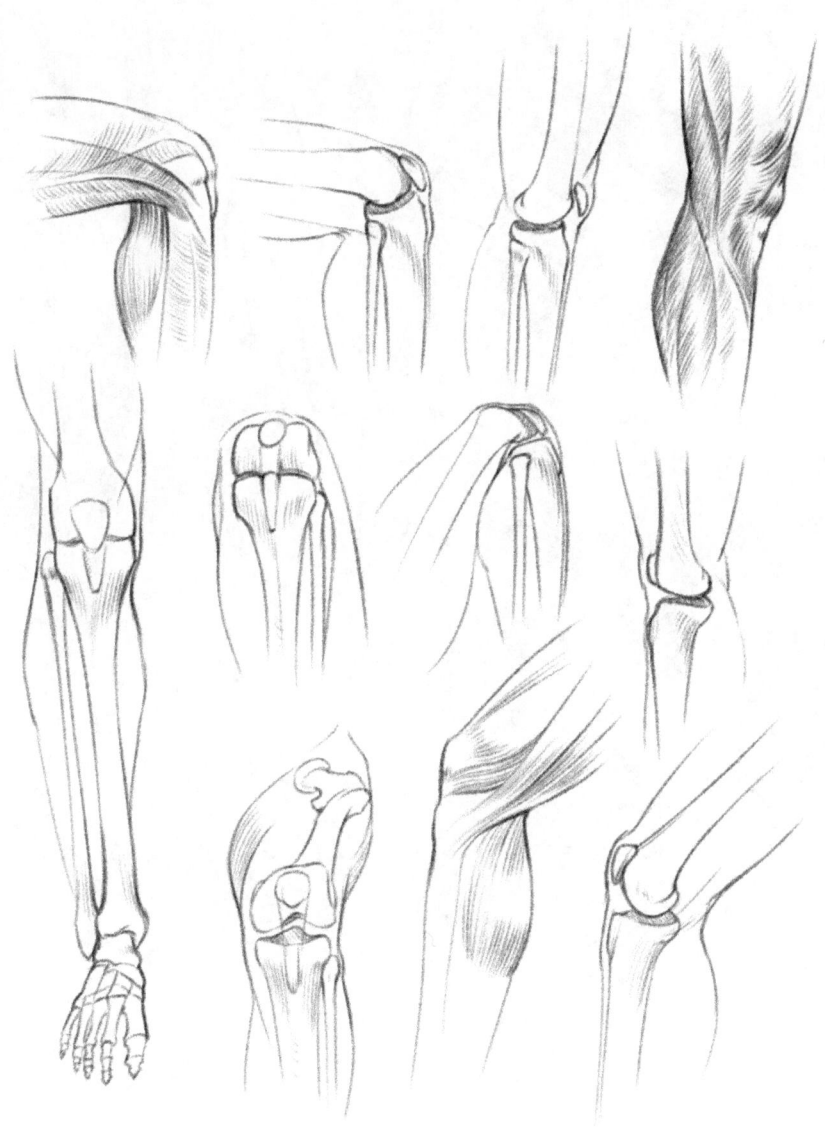

Features of movement of the knee joint. Pay attention to how the release of the patella changes when the leg is bent and the main muscle forms.

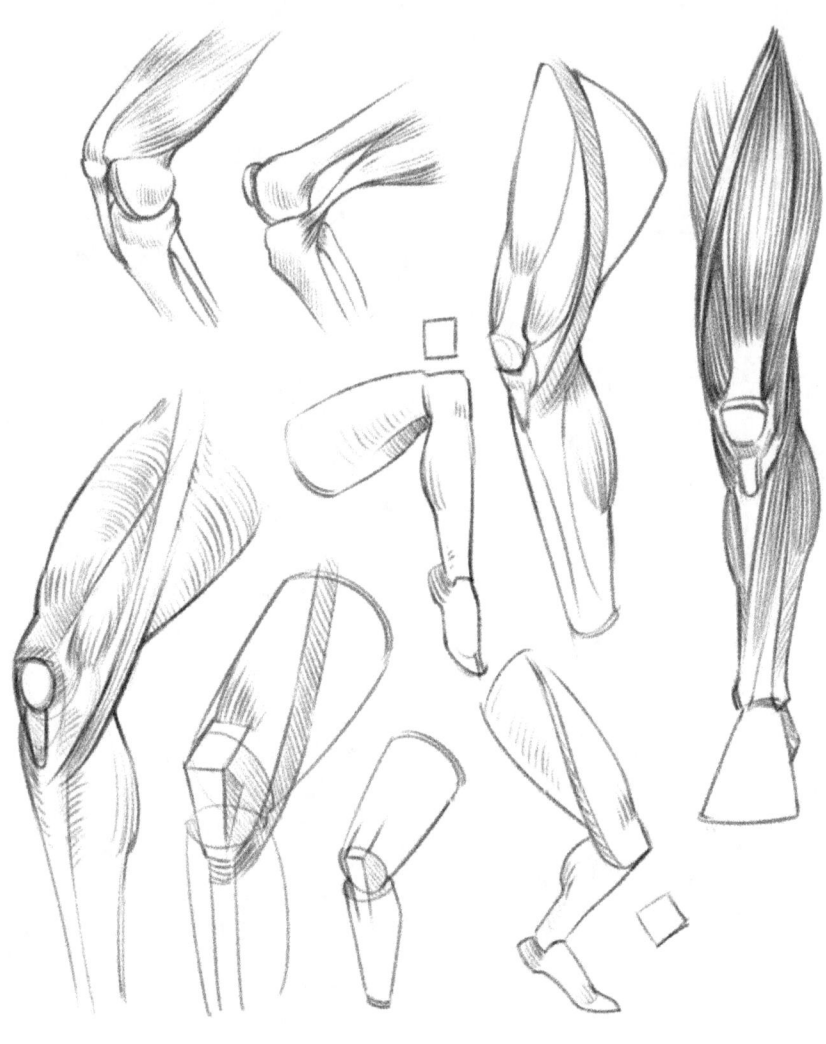

The knee joint is a complex structure, so it is worth analyzing its shape in more detail. When the leg is straight, the knee is slightly covered by muscular forms and stands out less. When the leg is bent at the knee, the kneecap rises up and forms a point that resembles a right angle. Therefore, we schematically depict the knee of the bent leg as sharp or more rounded and mark the patella.

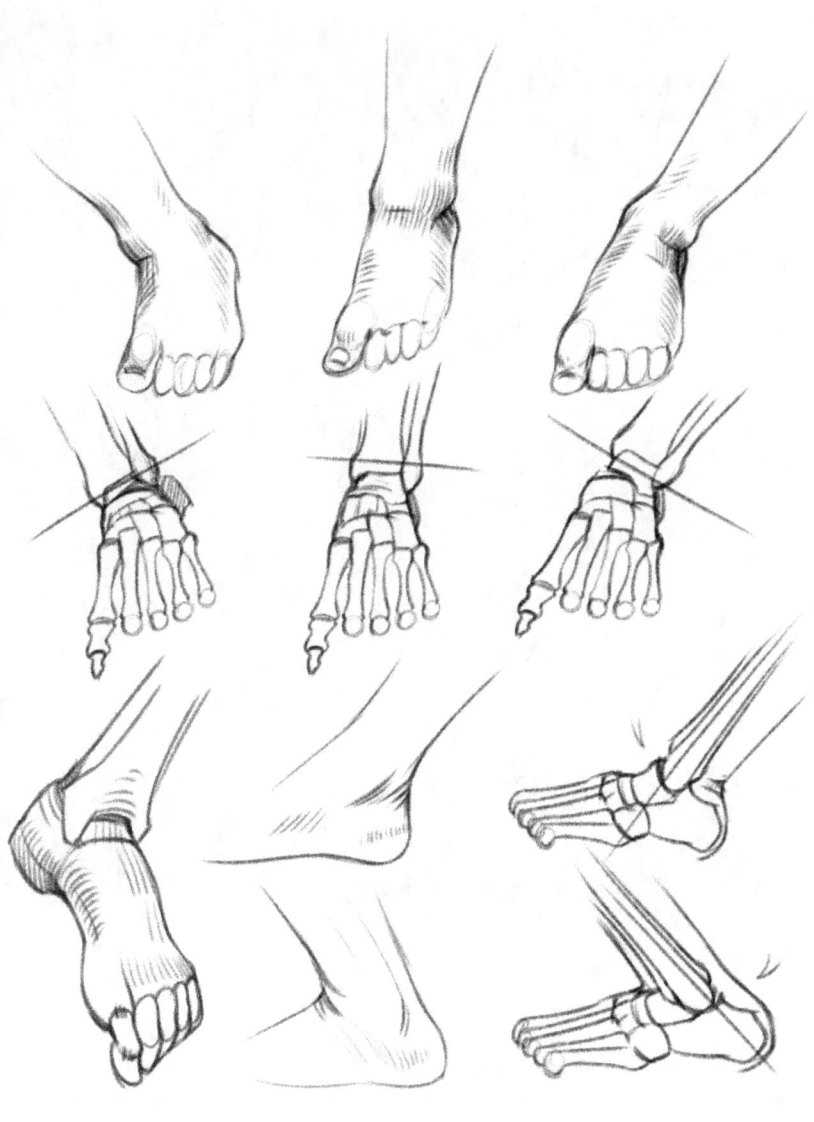

The ankle-foot joint has a special shape that ensures the mobility of the foot, as well as its balance and stability at various angles or turns of the foot.

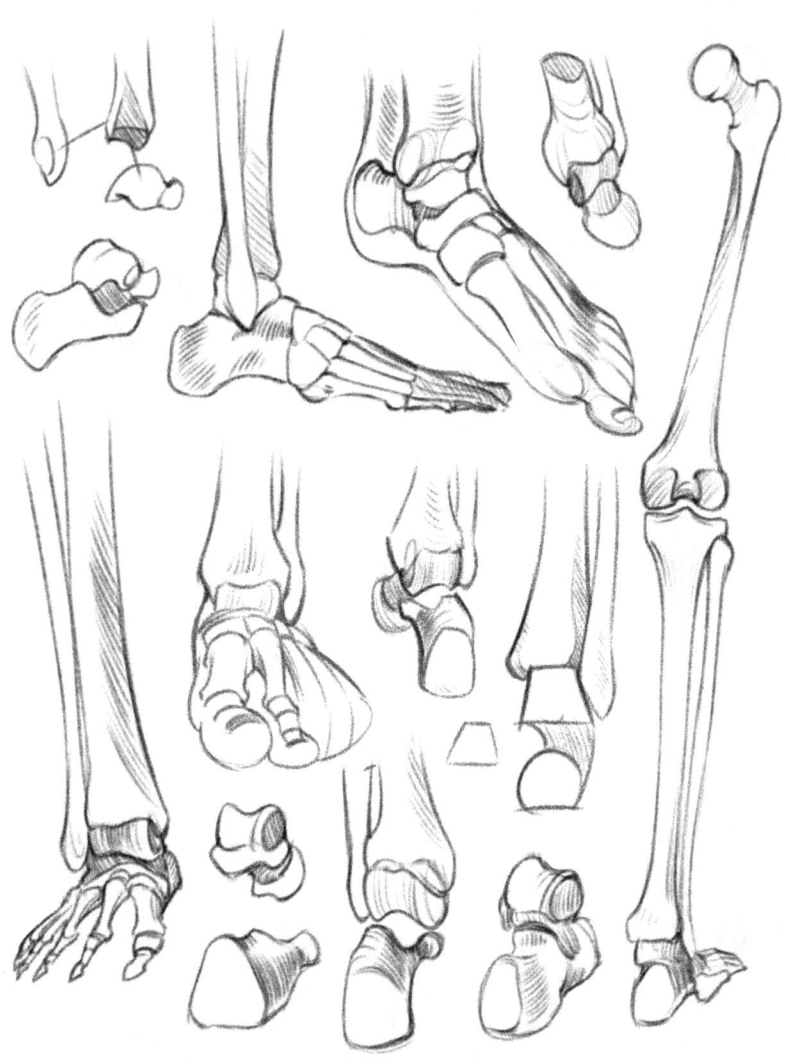

The back part of the human foot is formed by seven bones, which are called tarsus (lat. tarsus). The metatarsal is involved in the formation of the ankle joint, provides support for the foot, and forms the basis for the metatarsal bones.

Let's consider the largest ones first. The calcaneus is the largest bone of the foot, located in the rear part. It forms the base of the foot and provides support. The talus bone is located in front of the calcaneus. It participates in the formation of the ankle joint. The tibia bones frame it, forming a pincer.

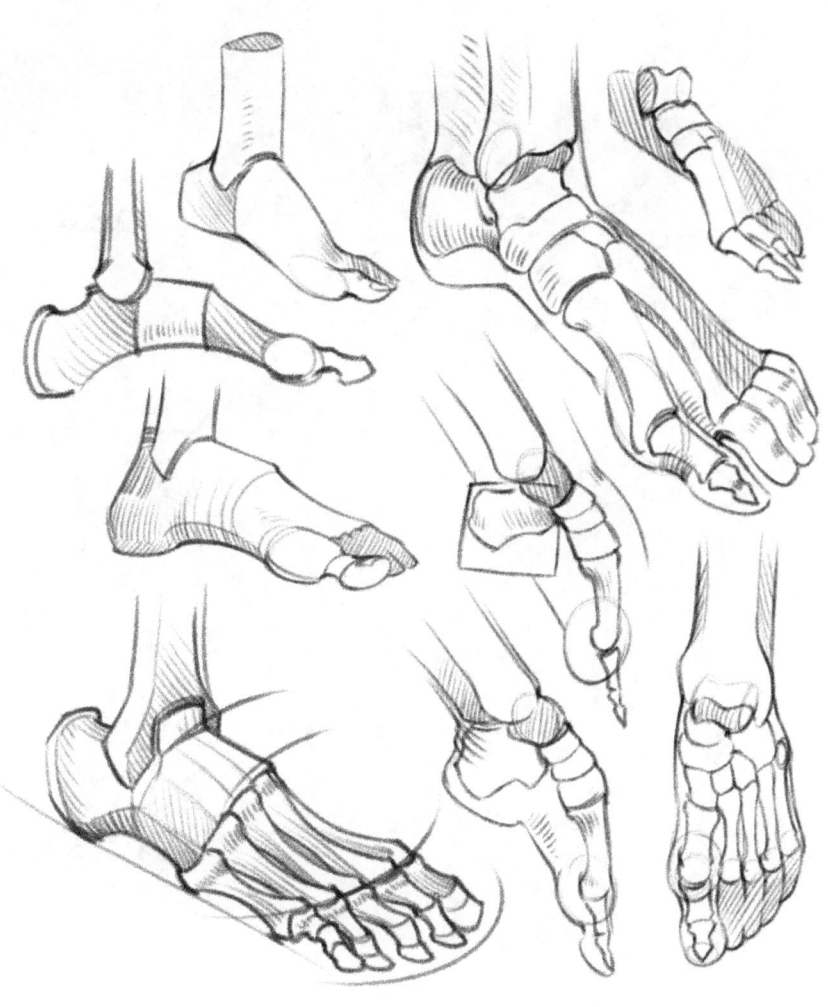

The navicular bone is located between the calcaneus and the talus. It is the key metatarsal bone that provides the connection between the front and back parts of the foot.

In front of the navicular bone is the cuboid bone. It forms the basis for the 4th and 5th metatarsal bones. Lateral, intermediate, and medial wedge-shaped bones are also distinguished. Visually, these bones form an arch.

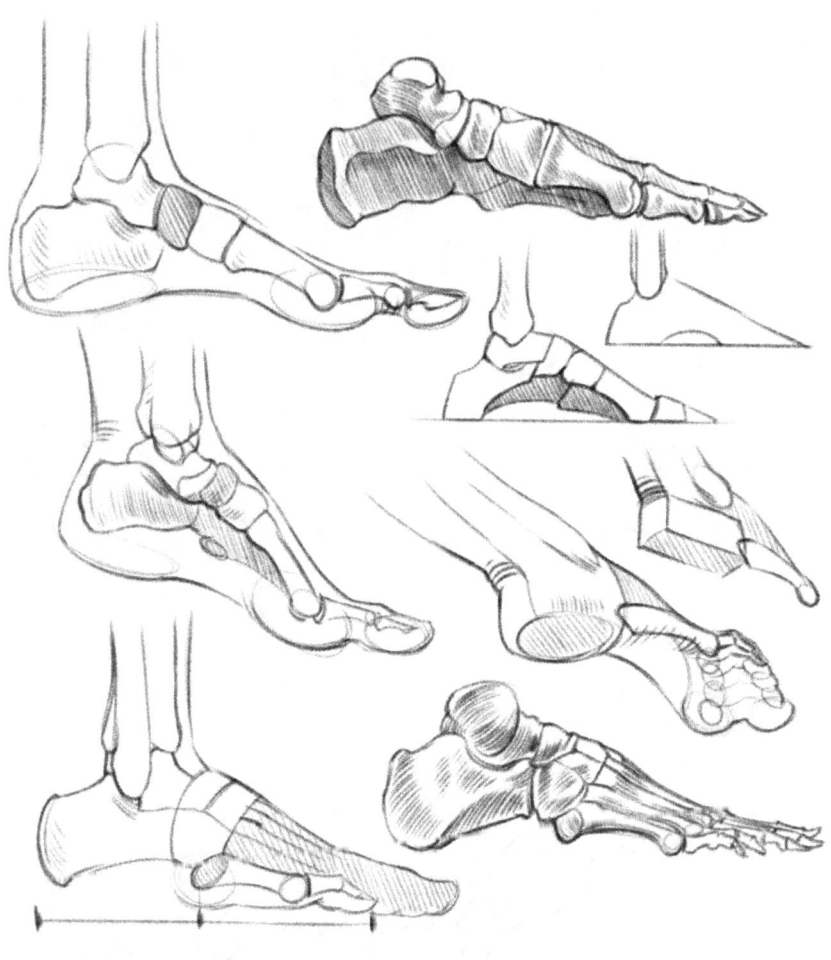

The metatarsal bones are connected by joints that provide foot mobility.

Visible extreme points can be distinguished on the inside and outside of the leg. Yes, internally a boat-shaped bone protrudes on the side, which is clearly visible when the foot is lowered or turned to the side. The joint of the thumb stands out the most, we will expand on it later.

On the outside, you can see the base of the metatarsal bone of the little finger. It is located in the middle of the distance from the heel to the end of the little finger and can be more rounded and visible depending on the position of the foot and its features.

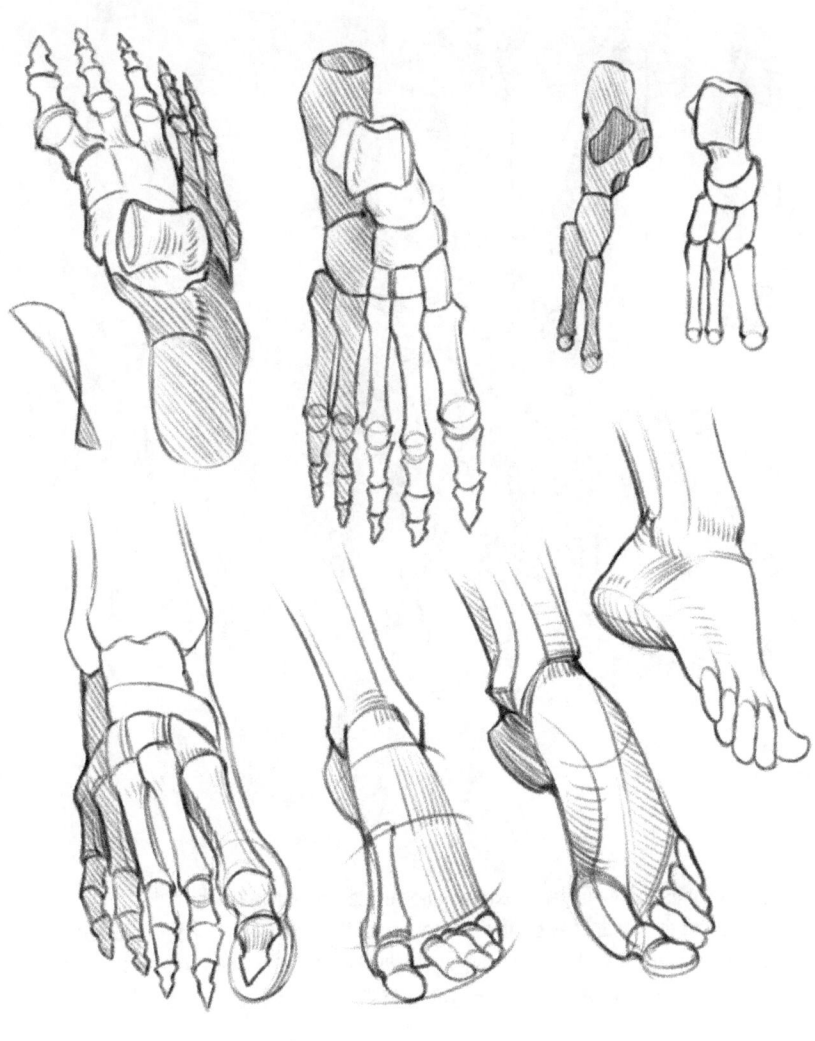

The inside of the foot is more dynamic and has a rise/bend. The outer side of the foot is completely on the surface and provides stable contact. In this way, we can divide the foot into raised and lowered parts (upper and lower), which characterize the features of the structure of the bones of the foot and its function.

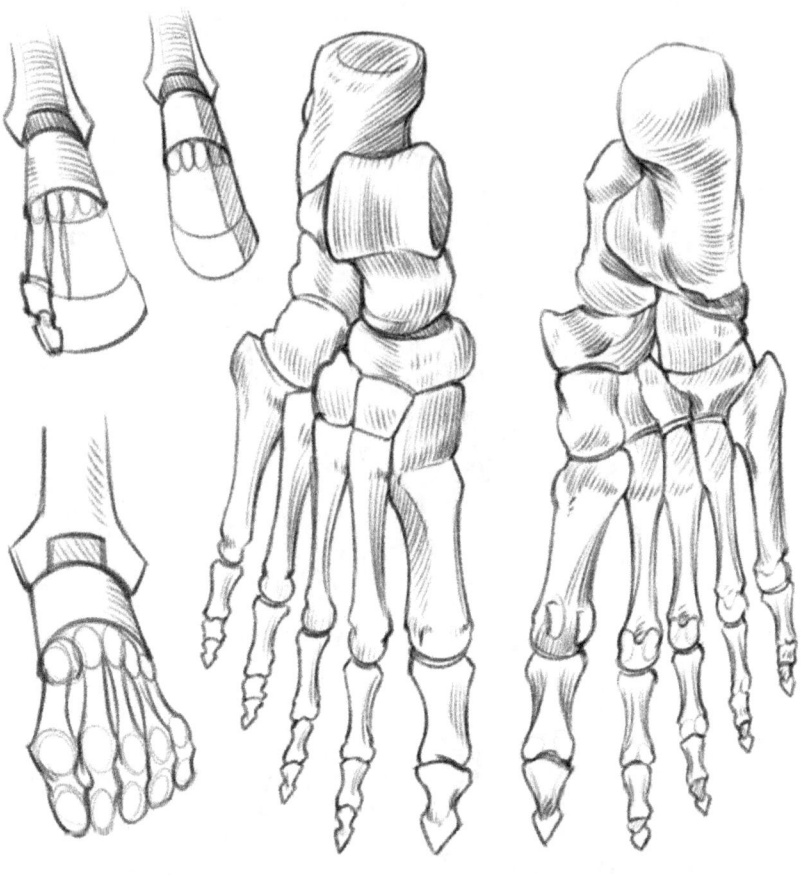

The phalanges of the fingers start from the metatarsal bones, which are located in the front part of the hand. They ensure the mobility of the fingers. In each finger, except for the big one, there are three phalanges: proximal (main), middle and distal (end). The thumb has only two phalanges: proximal and distal (as in fingers).

The phalanges have a cylindrical shape. They consist of a body and a head. The body of the phalanx has a thickened base and tapers to the head. The head of the phalanx has a spherical shape and has an articular surface that connects to the articular surface of the adjacent phalanx.

The largest phalanx bone is the head of the proximal phalanx of the thumb, and the smallest is the head of the distal phalanx of the little finger.

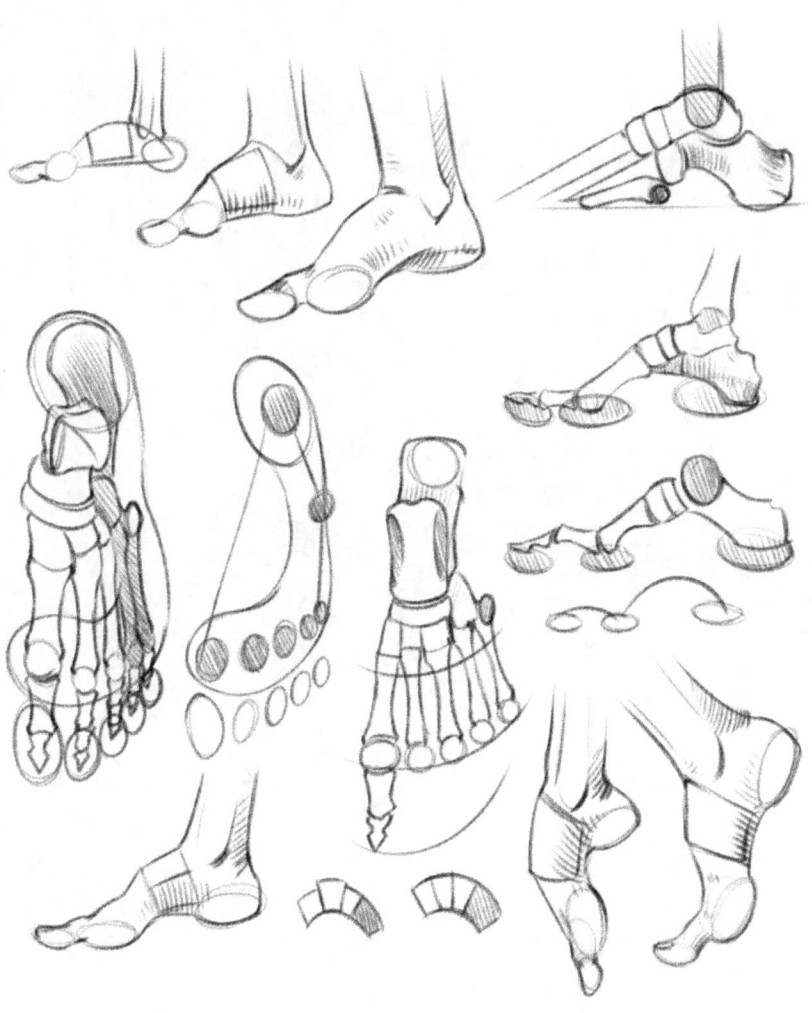

Let's consider the features of the structure of the legs in simple forms. The talus can be represented as a sphere that shows the mobility of the ankle.

The bones of the middle of the foot have a rise and form a plantar arch. The sole has volumetric masses on both sides - the pad and joint of the thumb on one side and the heel on the other. Features of the structure form the main points of contact of the foot with the surface. The ends of the metatarsal bones form a cushion at the front of the foot, the heel at the back, and the point of the base of the metatarsal bone of the little finger stands out from the outside.

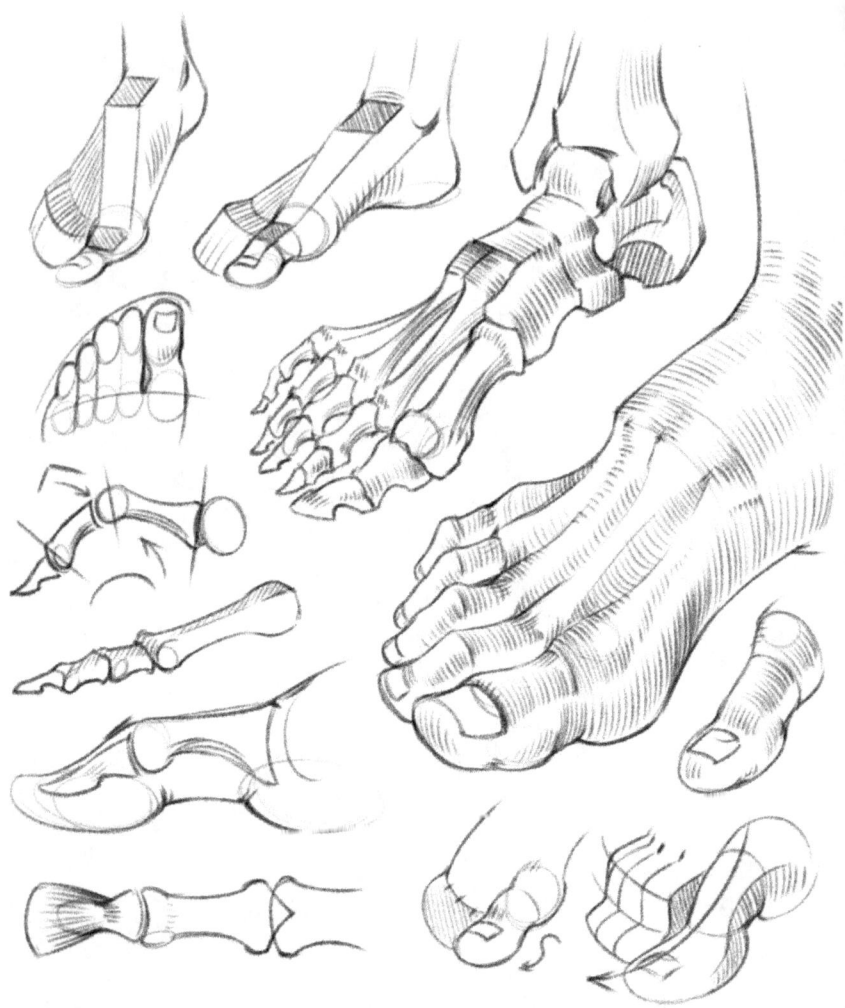

Toes are similar to each other but have a significant difference. The metatarsal bone of the thumb and the finger itself seems to be in a different plane from the other fingers. This is due to the fact that the metatarsal bone of the thumb is located at a different angle than the metatarsal bones of the other fingers. This angle allows the thumb to perform movements that are not possible for other fingers. For example, the thumb can bend to the sides, which allows us to hold objects.

In addition, the head of the proximal phalanx of the thumb has a larger head than the heads of the proximal phalanges of the other fingers. It also promotes greater mobility in the thumb.

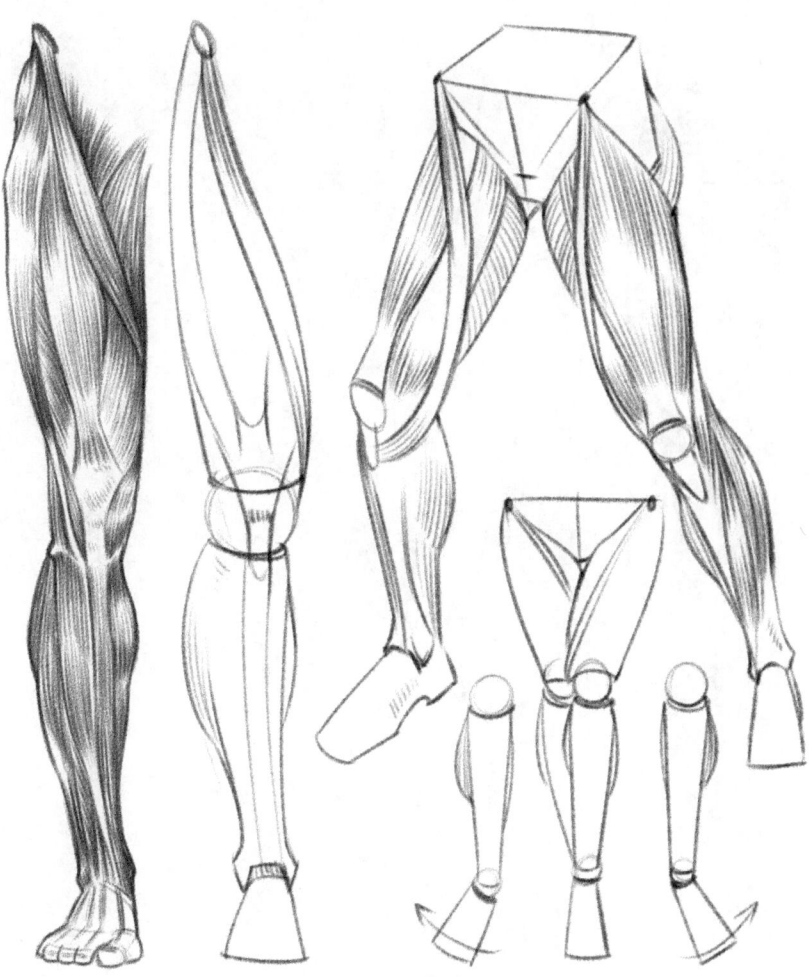

The basic shape of the leg is formed by the massive quadriceps at the front of the thigh and the calf at the back of the lower leg. The tibialis anterior muscle of the lower leg is less visible, so we do not mark it.

From the top from the outer point of the thigh to the inner a diagonal line (brachioradialis) passes on the sides of the knee, which is well distinguished on the legs in tension or movement.

Depending on the movements of the legs, the muscles are either flatter and stretched or more tense and sharper. Pay attention to how the general shape of the lower leg changes relative to the inclination of the foot.

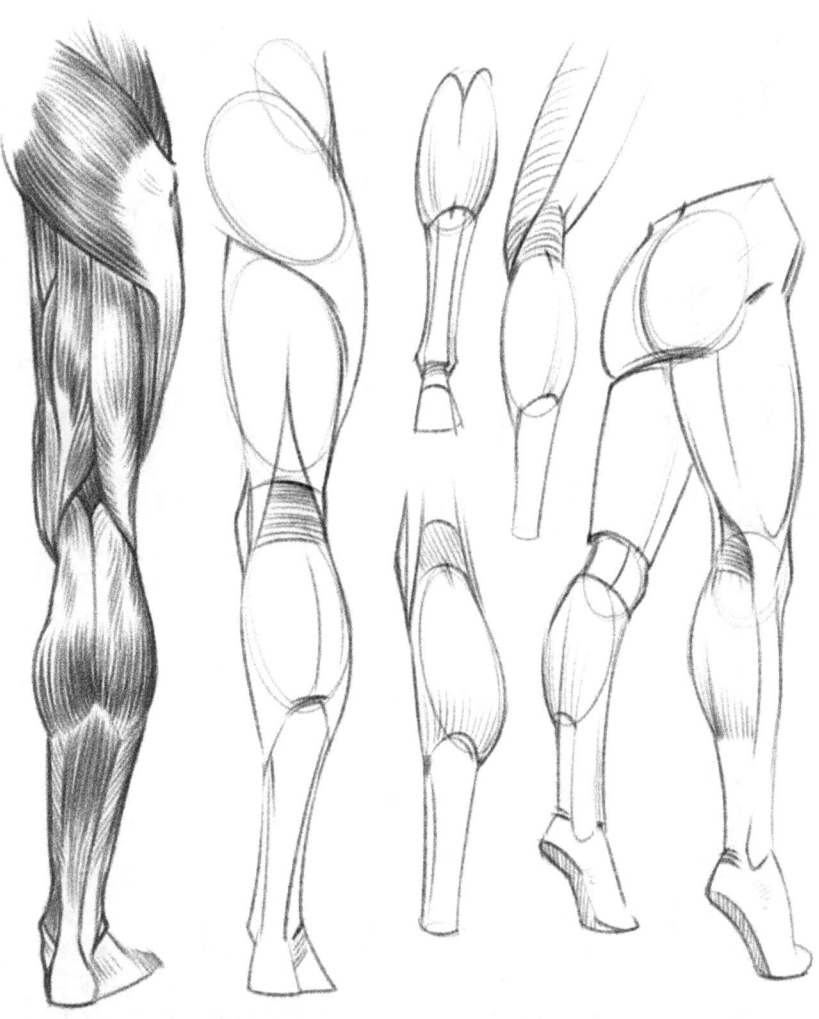

The most prominent muscle of the back of the leg is the calf muscle - an important muscle that provides mobility of the lower leg. It allows us to walk, run, jump, stand on tiptoes, and perform other leg movements. It is a superficial muscle, so it is clearly visible under the skin. The calf muscle resembles an egg-shaped shape, divided into 2 parts.

The semitendinosus and biceps muscles of the thigh are attached to the triceps of the arm. They cover the knee from both sides and form a hole under the knee.

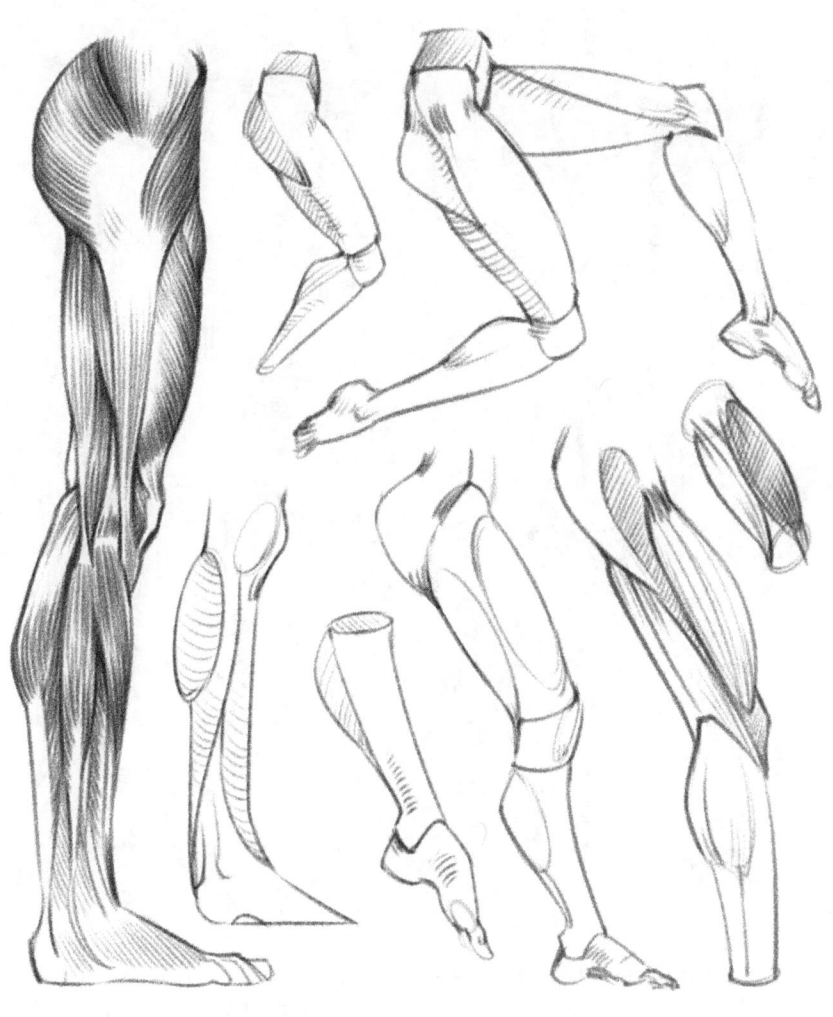

From the outside of the thigh, the large gluteal muscle extends to the knee and creates a flat line that divides the thigh into front and back parts. Therefore, from the side, the thigh can be depicted as a cylinder divided in two, or add 2 muscular rounded shapes in front and back.

Laterally, the shin can be divided into 3 muscle groups - the main oval shape at the back (calf) and less visible muscles at the front and back that cover the bone. They form a long fossa parallel to the fibula.

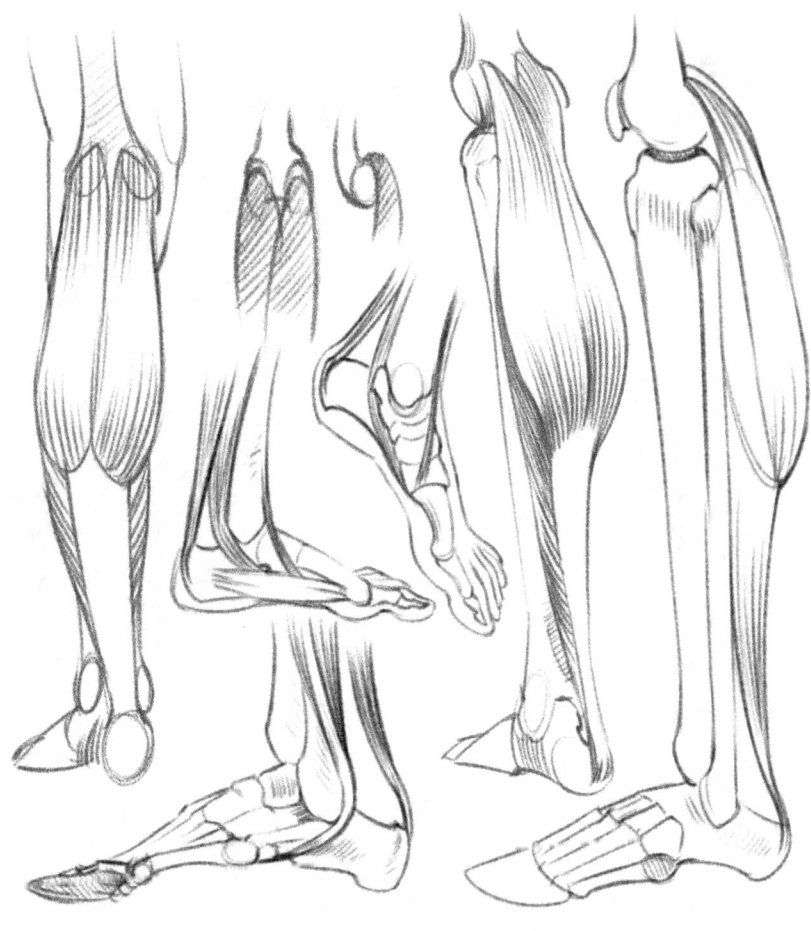

The calf consists of two powerful fleshy heads - medial and lateral. The medial head is located closer to the middle of the leg, and the lateral head is closer to the outer edge. It is attached from above to the medial and lateral sides of the femur (in its lower back part).

The heads of the calf muscle are connected to a common tendon band, which ends at the calcaneus (Achilles tendon).

Most of the muscles of the lower leg end on the bones of the foot and ensure its mobility. For example, the plantar muscle (musculus planlaris), which stretches the capsule of the knee joint when bending and rotating the lower leg.

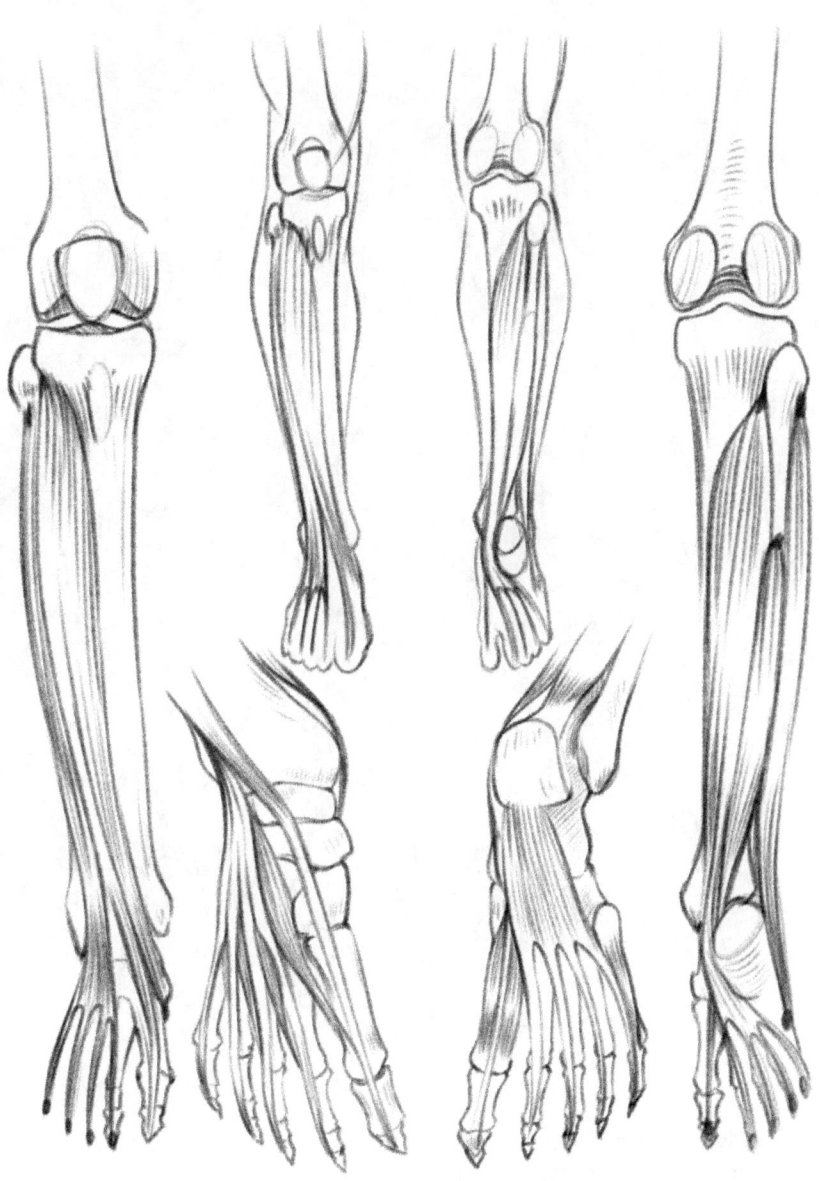

The muscles responsible for flexion and extension of the toes can be divided into two groups - flexors and extensors. The flexor muscles are located on the lateral and plantar surfaces of the foot and start from the back of the lower leg. The extensor muscles are located on the upper surface of the foot and open from the front side of the lower leg.

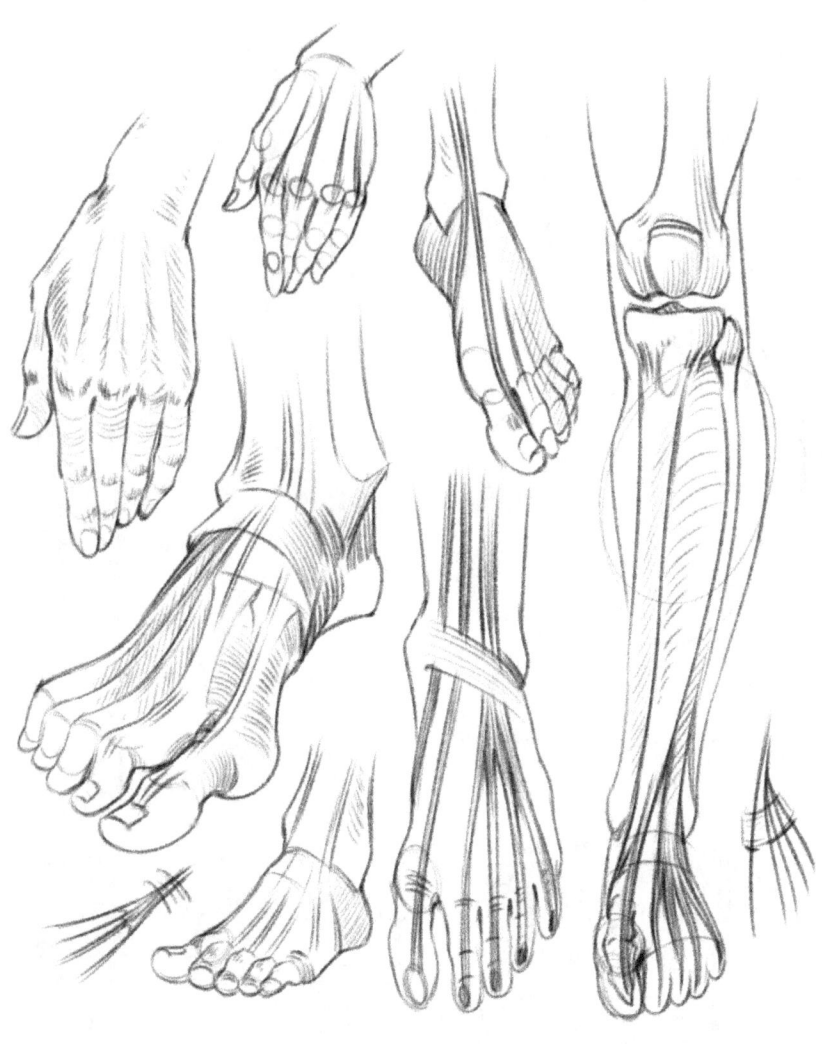

The lines on the top of the foot are called tendon lines. They are formed by the tendons of the muscles that are responsible for extending the toes. The flexor of the thumb is separate, while the other superficial flexors of the fingers are united.

The tendon lines of the foot resemble the structure of the back of the hand, which is also responsible for the movement and extension of the fingers.

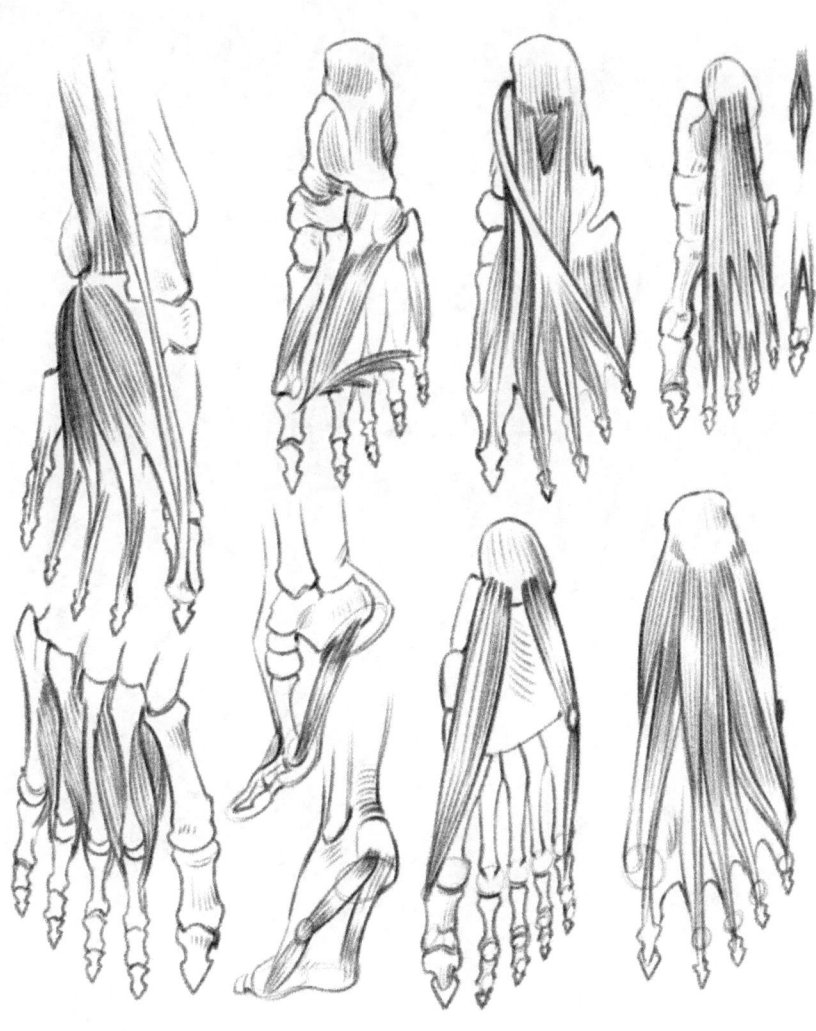

Image of the main muscles of the foot, superficial and internal. They are responsible for the movement of the toes, as well as for maintaining the foot in the correct position. The extensor muscles of the toes are located in the front part of the foot and are responsible for extending the toes. The toe flexor muscles are located at the bottom of the foot and are responsible for bending the toes. The interosseous muscles are located between the bones of the foot and are responsible for the movement of the toes. It is important that the muscles that provide movement of the thumb are separate, as well as some muscles of the little finger.

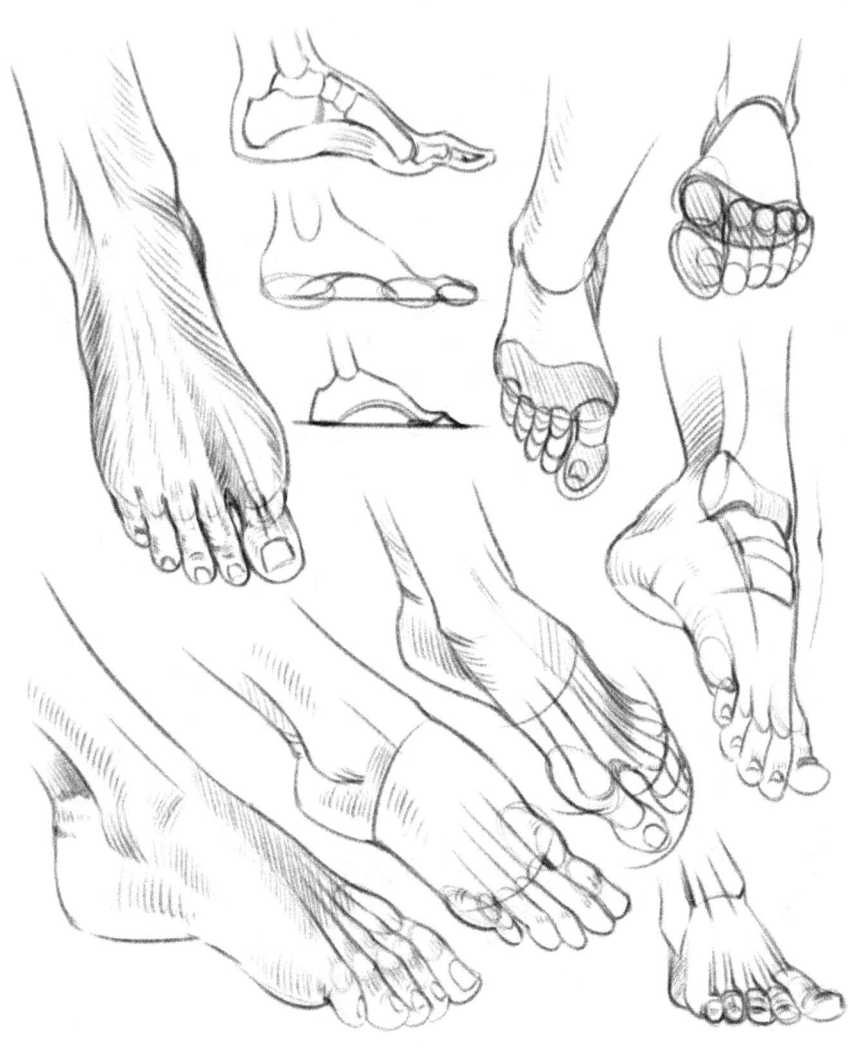

Consider the appearance of the foot based on its internal structure. Tendon lines repeat the distribution of the fingers and stretch to the lower leg. They are more visible in the part of the metatarsal bones, above the arch of the middle foot they have a smoother shape (but with the leg extended, the hole formed by the protrusion of the talus bone is visible).

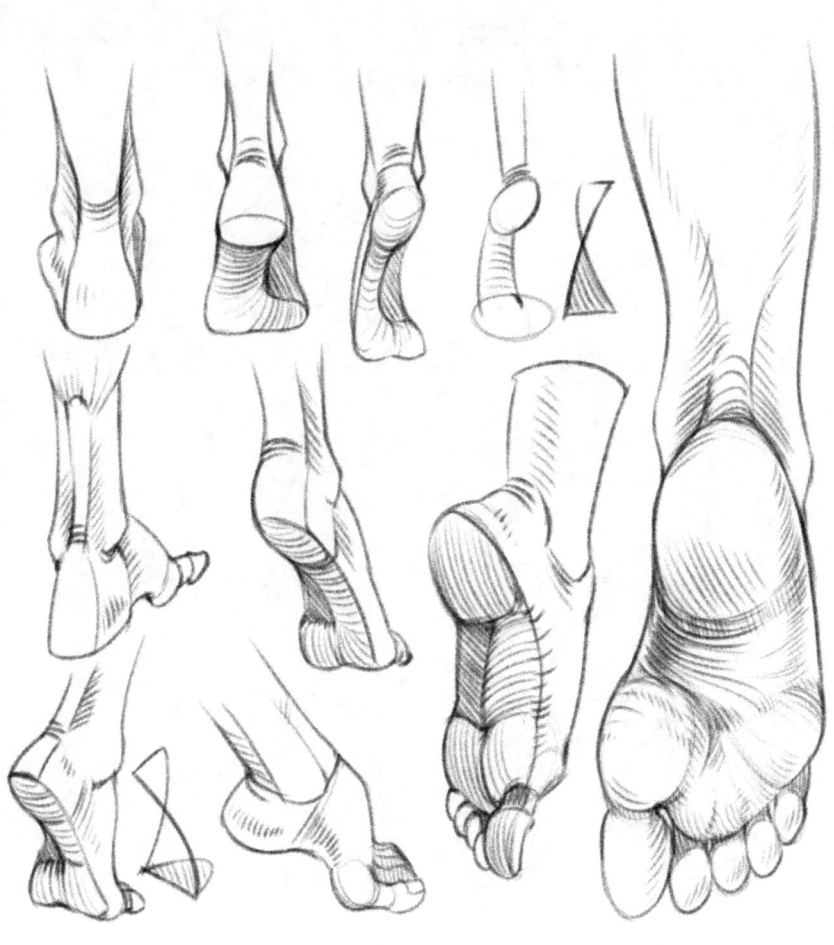

The back of the foot resembles an hourglass. The shape behind the Achilles tendon narrows to the heel and expands, repeating the shape of the heel. In the narrowest part, we often see folds of skin that are formed when the heel is directed towards the lower leg. On both sides, we can see protrusions - the ends of the large and small tibia.

When the heel is raised, we can clearly see the bent plane of the foot. Cushions on the heel and under the end of the metatarsal bones create additional volume in the front and back of the foot.

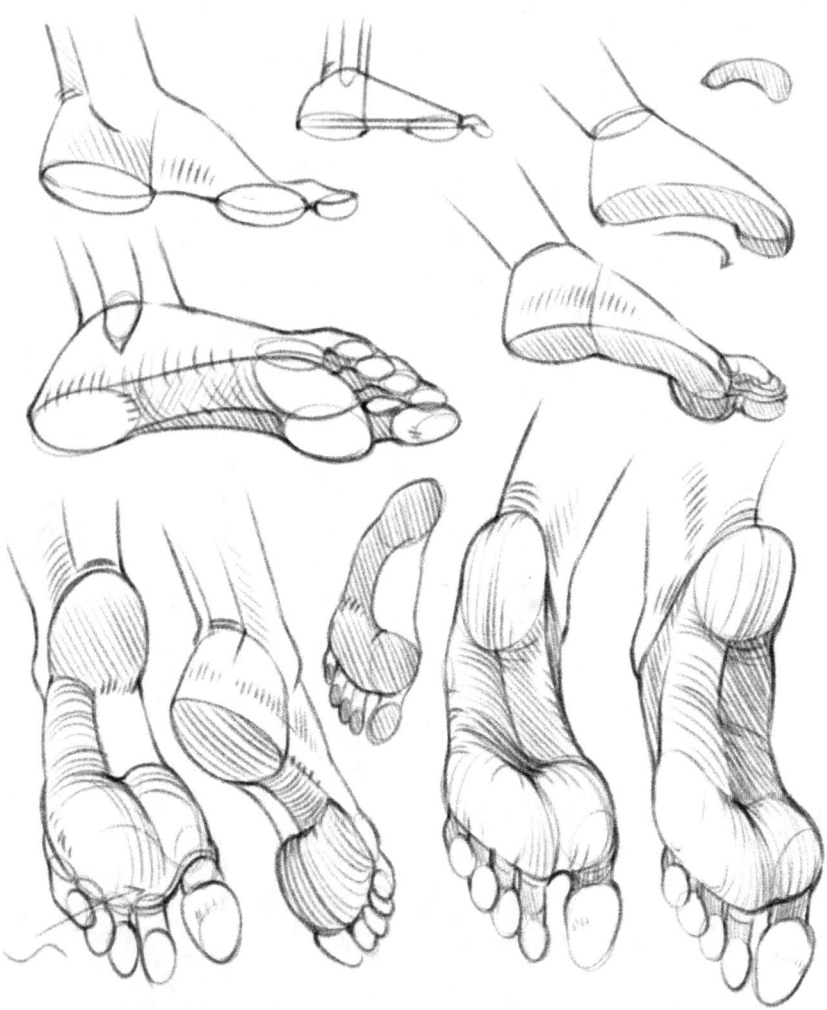

The volumetric masses of the sole are a layer of fatty tissue that cushions the foot, improves adhesion to the surface, and provides the function of thermal insulation. Fat masses of the sole are located mainly under the toes, under the heel, and along the outer edge of the foot. The general shape resembles the letter "C" - two rounded shapes that are connected to each other on the outside of the foot.

The shape of fat masses on the sole of the foot depends on the amount of adipose tissue, the shape of the bones of the foot, and the size and position of the muscles. For example, when we stand on our heels, the fat masses under the heel are compressed, and the fat masses under the toes are stretched. When we walk, the fat masses of the sole of the foot are constantly changing their shape to provide shock absorption and traction on the surface.

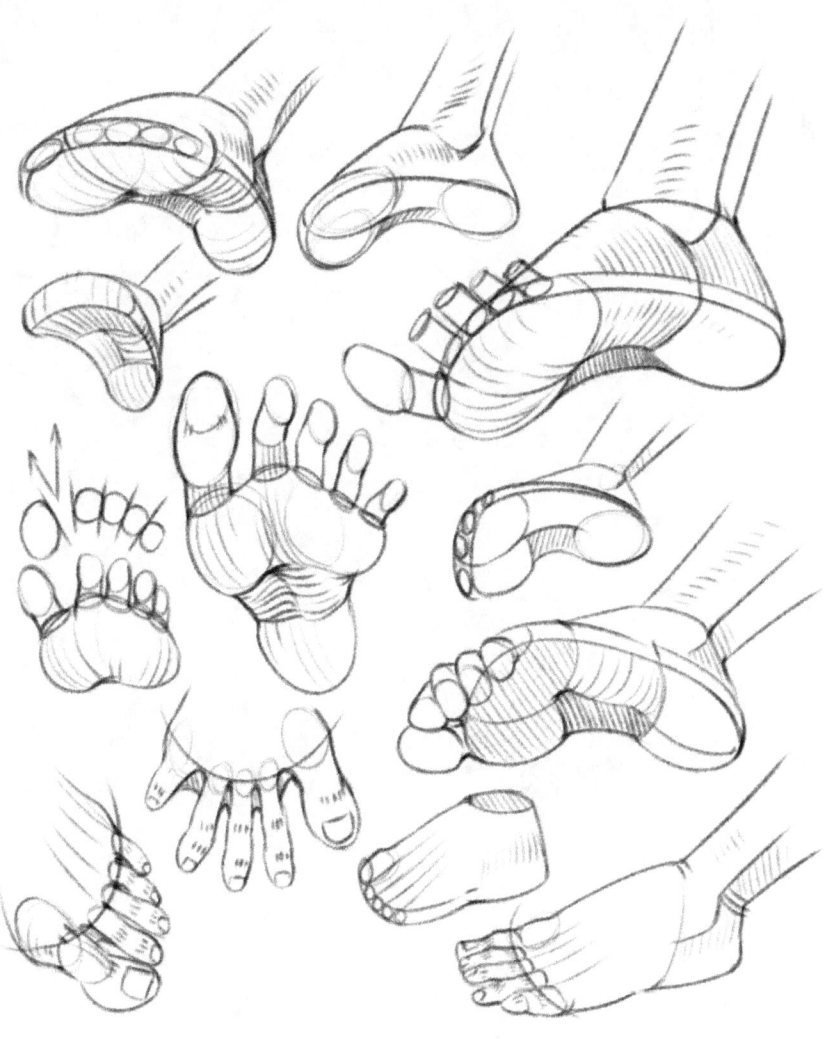

The knuckle of the fingers is divided into 2 parts, because the joint of the thumb is much larger than the others and strongly stands out. This pad is rounded and marks a conventional arc, which makes it easier for the artist to determine the beginning of the fingers. The extreme points of the fingers repeat the arc-shaped shape.

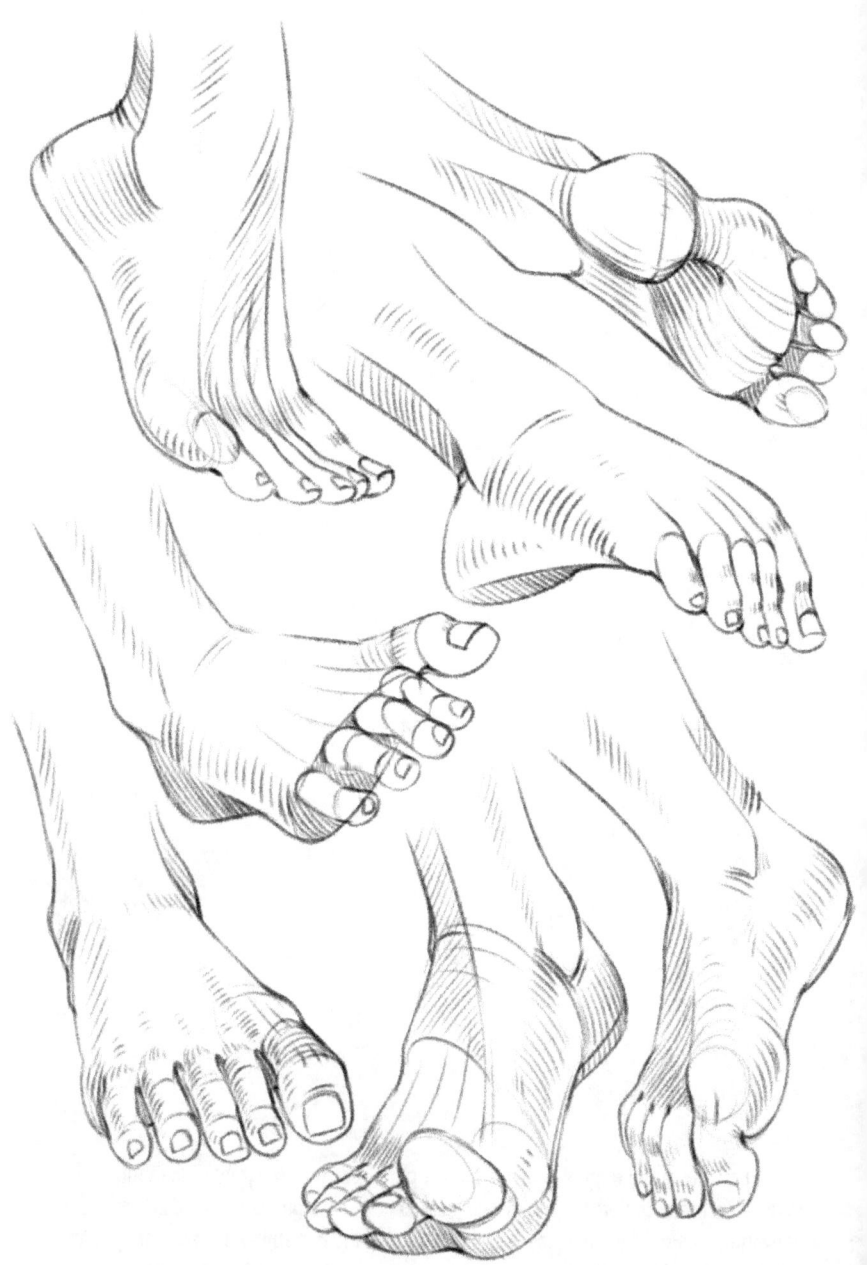

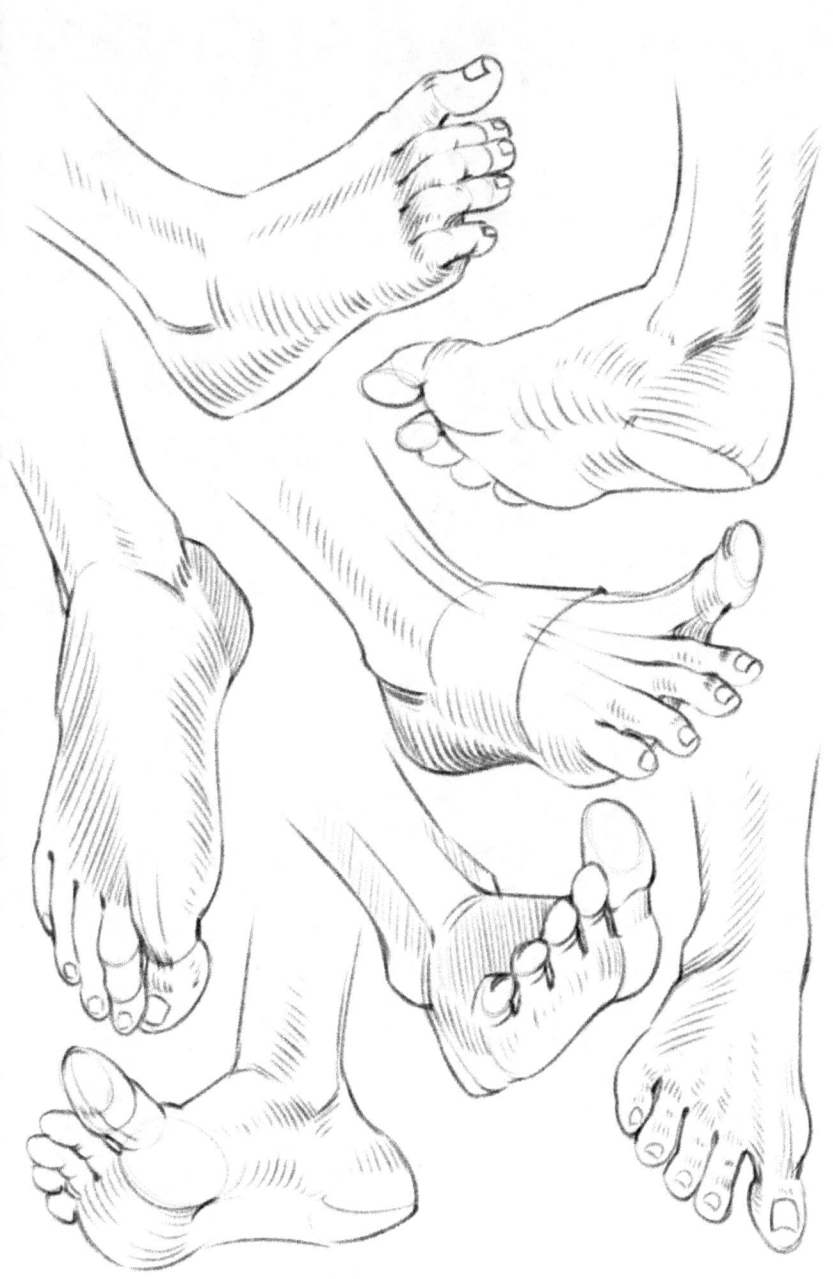

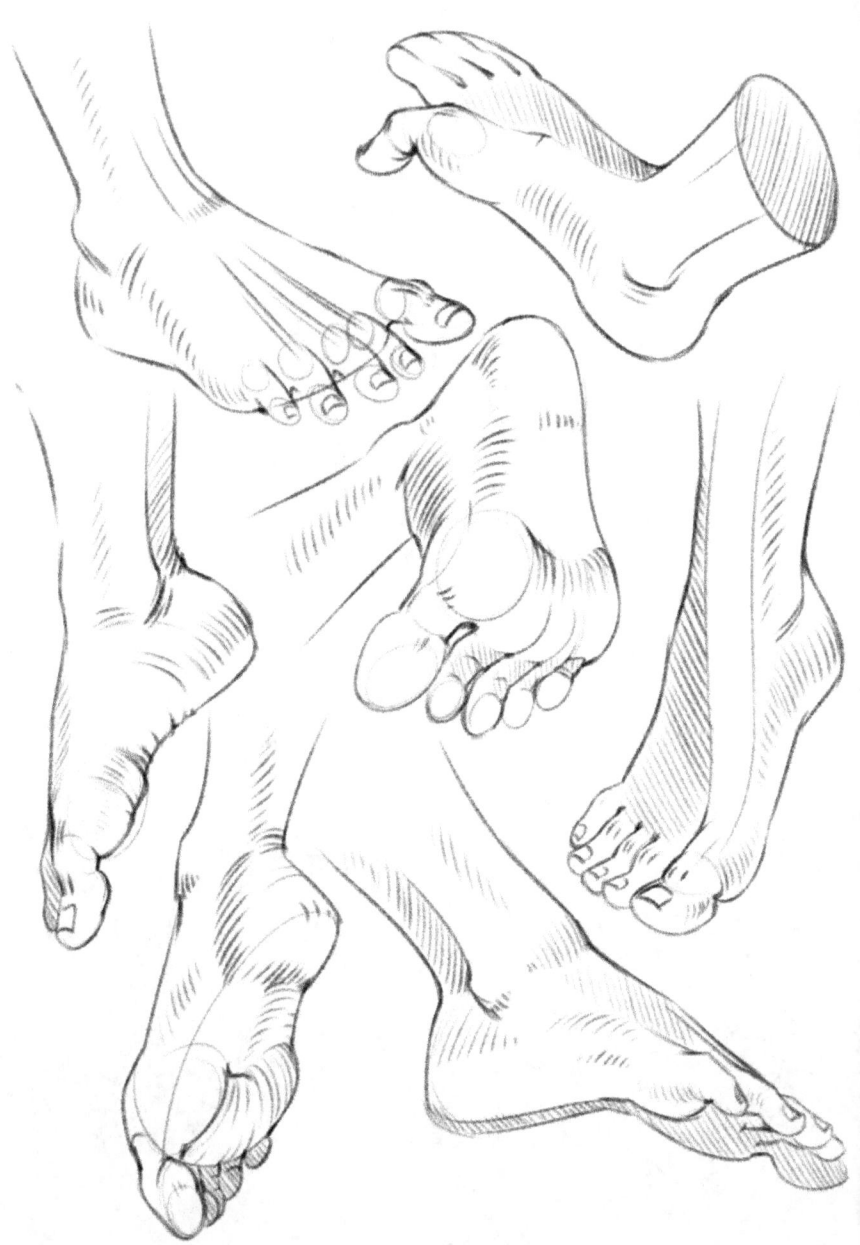

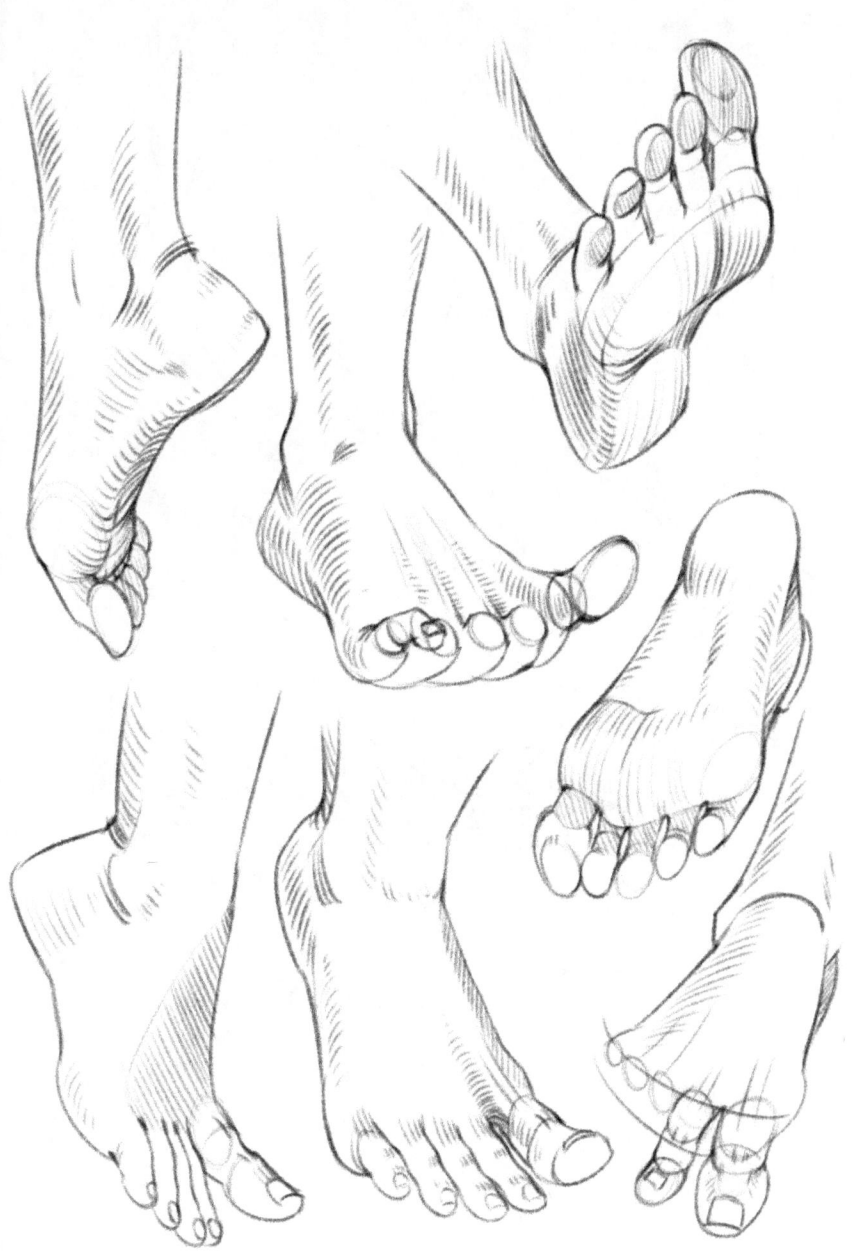

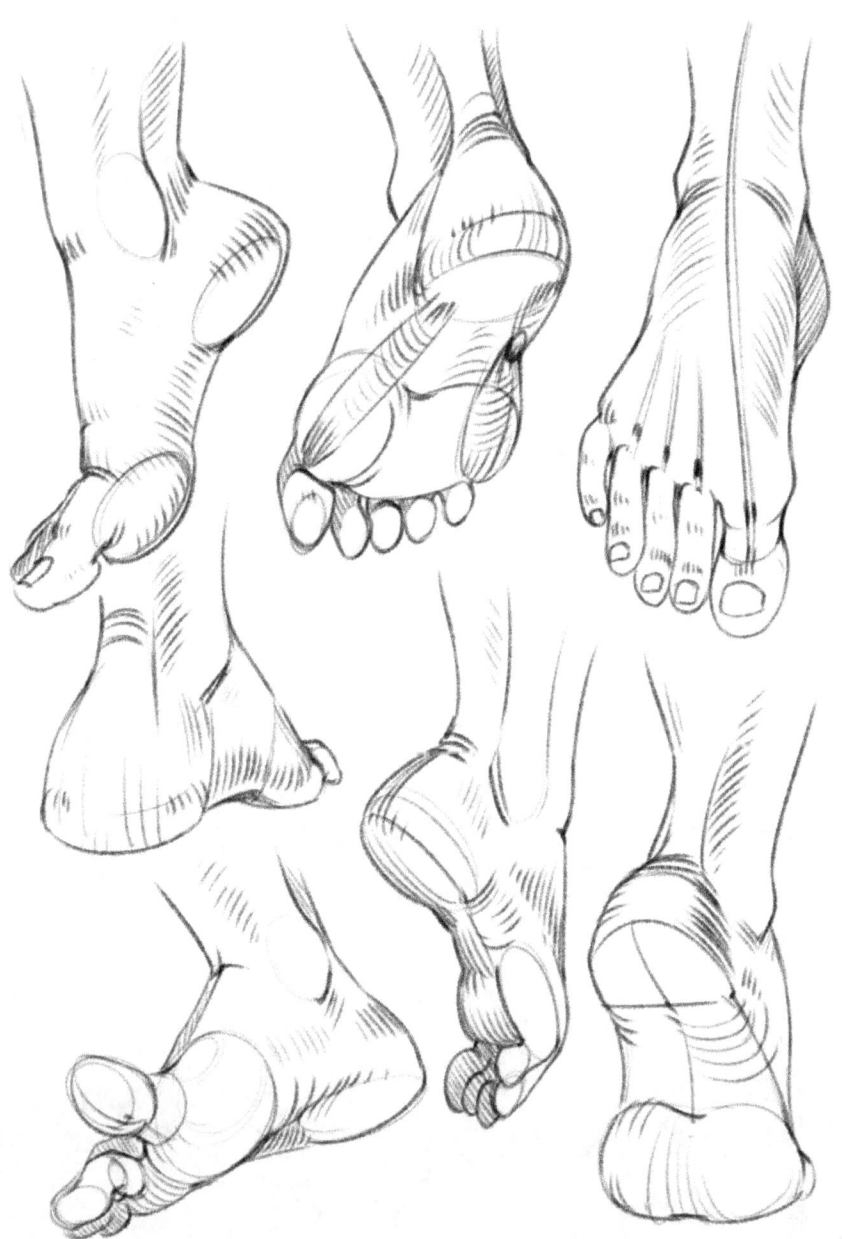

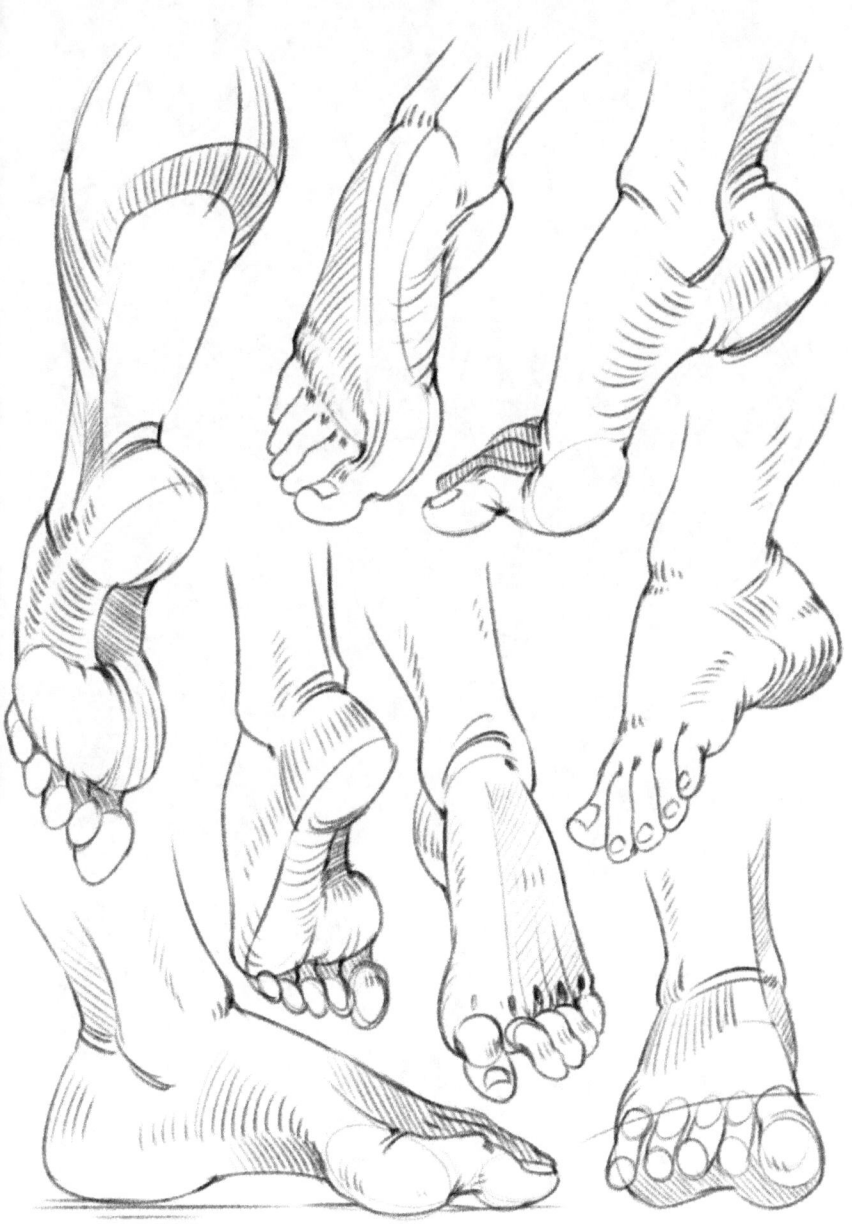

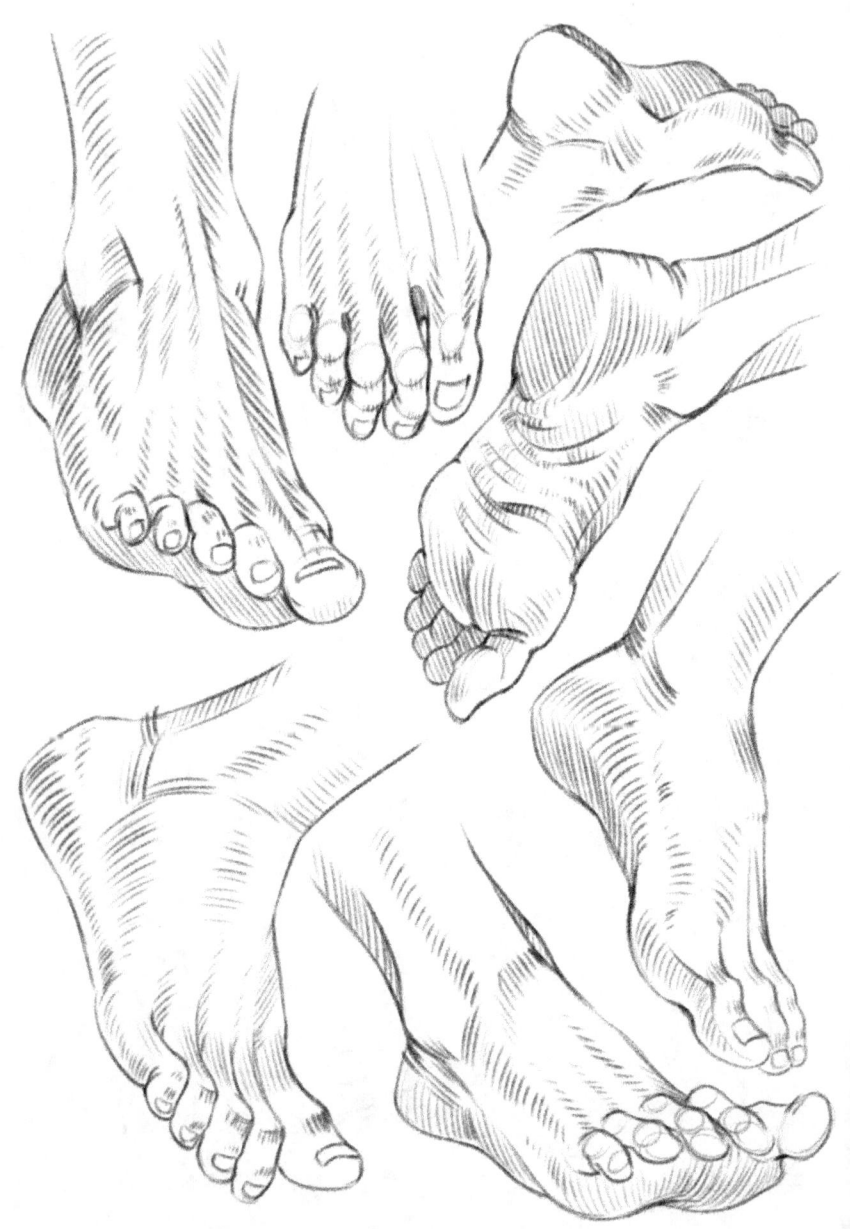

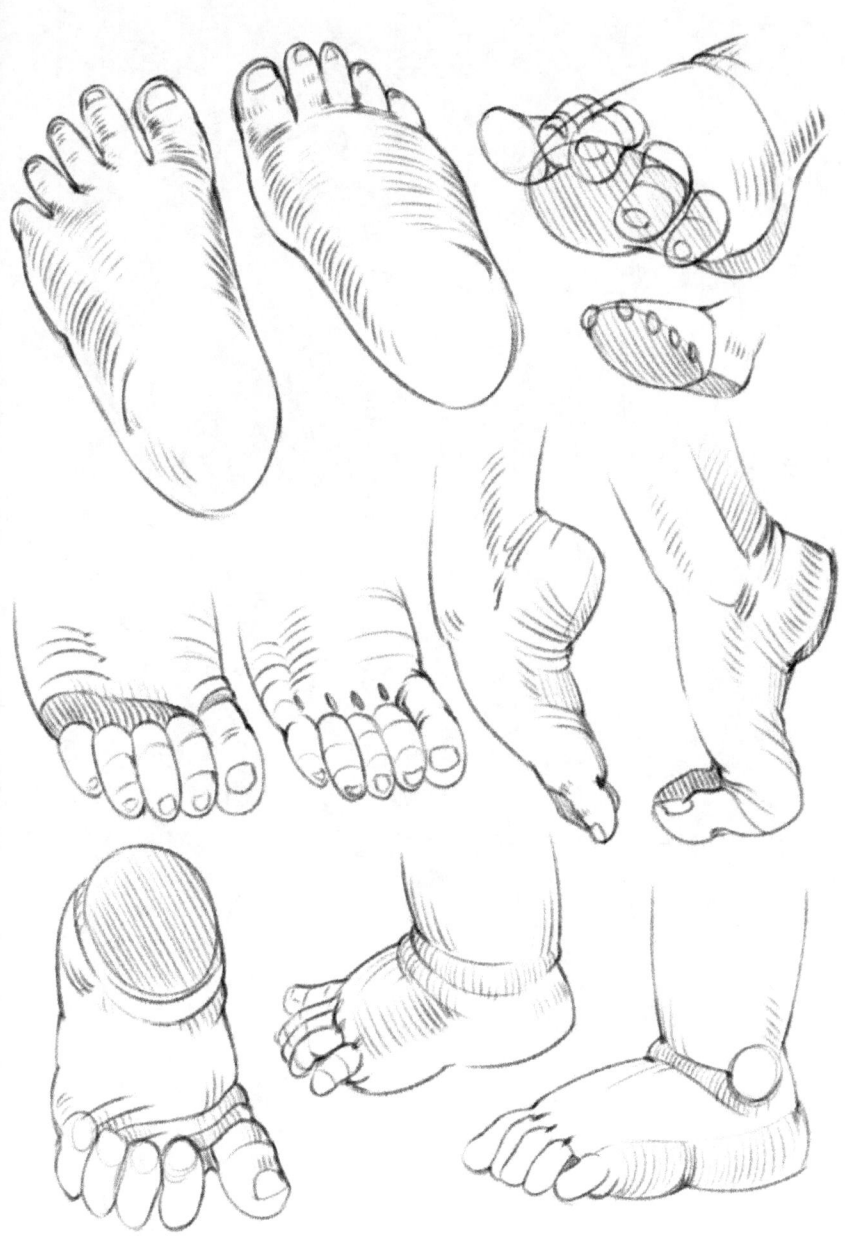

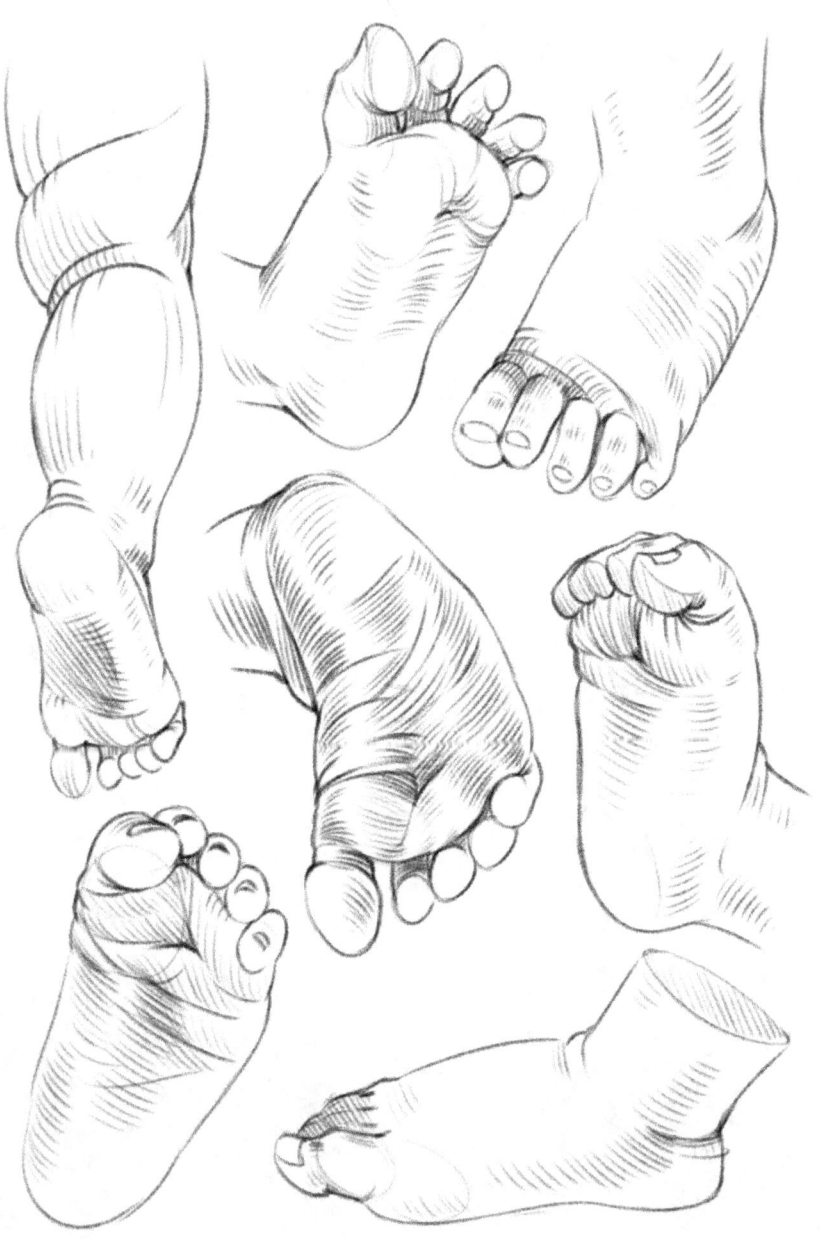

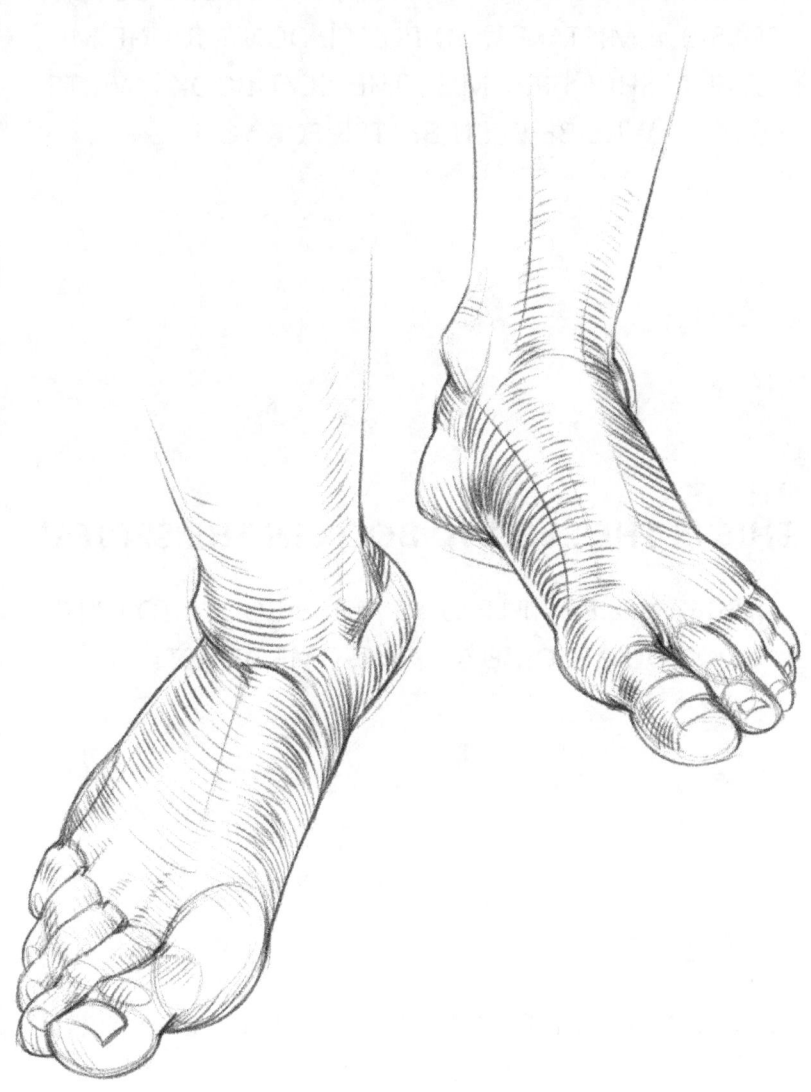

Oh, I hope you enjoyed the book! This is my **second** book and I'm very nervous about possible mistakes. So please don't judge me too harshly. I promise the next book I write will be even better for you!

THIS IS THE SECOND BOOK IN THE SERIES!

There will be at least 6 more books to help you become an awesome artist!

Look for more of my books on Amazon with this search:

DRAWIX

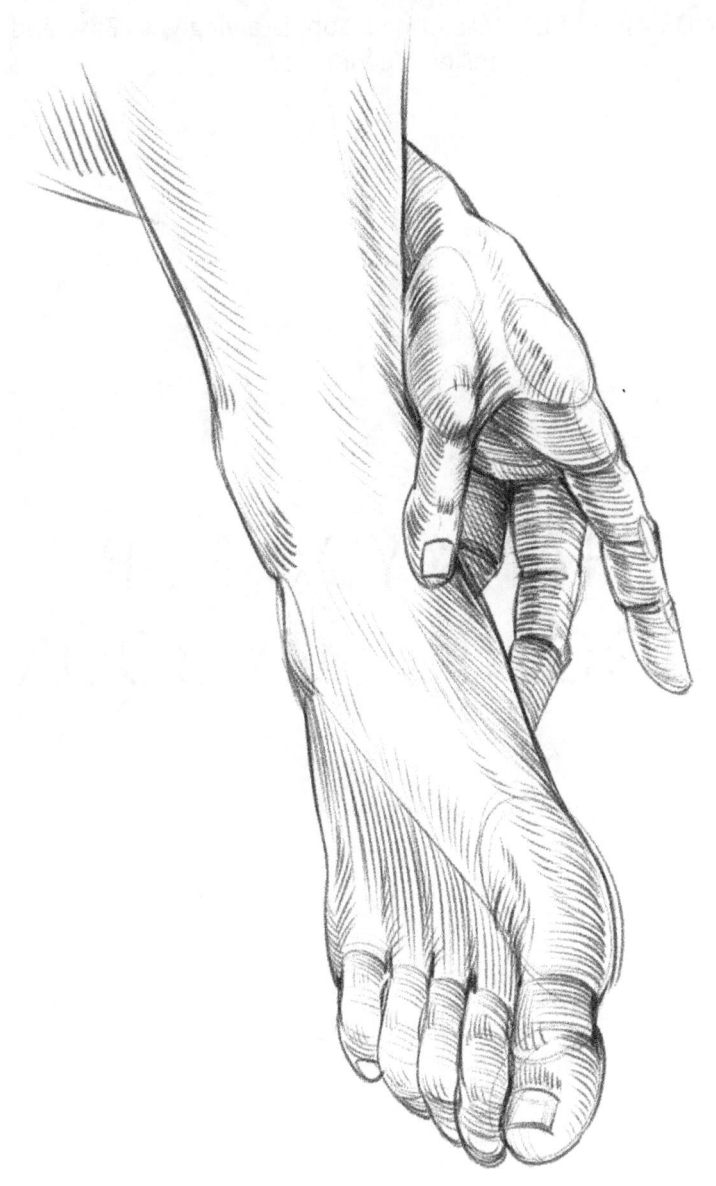

DRAWIX

HANDS AND FEET: Mastering Figure Drawing with Ease and Insider Techniques

THANK YOU FOR CHOOSING MY BOOK

ERICK KELLY

www.ingramcontent.com/pod-product-compliance
Lightning Source LLC
Chambersburg PA
CBHW070156230526
45471CB00002B/684